equal[ity]

compassion

consent

enlightenment

science

freedom

progress

"It is not necessary to be a Christian to appreciate the force of Glen Scrivener's argument in this punchy, engaging and entertaining book."

TOM HOLLAND, Historian; Author, *Dominion: How the Christian Revolution Remade the World*

"Brilliant, fascinating, readable and winsome! Glen Scrivener's *The Air We Breathe* powerfully demonstrates how Christianity has shaped our Western values so much that we don't even notice it. Highly recommended for skeptics, inquirers, believers, doubters and anyone wondering whether following Jesus still makes sense in the modern world."

GAVIN ORTLUND, Author, *Why God Makes Sense in a World That Doesn't*

"*The Air We Breathe* is a pithy, energetic and compelling exploration of how Christianity has formed our moral thinking—whether we realize it or not—and why the truth or falsehood of Christianity matters for all of us today. Whatever your current beliefs, I highly recommend you give Glen Scrivener a hearing!"

REBECCA McLAUGHLIN, Author, *Confronting Christianity*

"*The Air We Breathe* is a tour de force. Compressing 2,000 years of Western history into a couple of hundred pages, Glen has provided a brilliant summary of why the moral vision of the West is still fundamentally shaped by the Christian revolution. This is a must-read for any intellectually engaged person who is committed to human rights, compassion and progress but hasn't yet been introduced to the one who inspired the values they believe in."

JUSTIN BRIERLEY, Host, Premier's *Unbelievable?* Radio Show and Podcast; Author, *Unbelievable? Why, After Ten Years of Talking with Atheists, I'm Still a Christian*

"Glen Scrivener does an outstanding job of showing us that the Western world is not nearly as post-Christian as we tend to think. The evidence and fruit of biblical influence is all around us—even our unbelief is more Christian than we might realise. This is an eye-opening and game-changing book."

SAM ALLBERRY, Author; Speaker

"A really excellent book. The last time I read apologetics this compelling, it was by CS Lewis."

STEVE HOLMES, Senior Lecturer in Theology, University of St Andrews

"Secular Westerners reject Christian belief while feasting on its fruit. Whether the subject is enlightenment or equality, compassion or consent, science or freedom or progress, our neighbors have Christianity to thank for the values they cherish. This argument is provocative, and demonstrably true. Building on groundbreaking historical scholarship, Glen Scrivener has made a case that cannot be ignored. This is one of the most important books I've read in a long time."

MATT SMETHURST, Lead Pastor, River City Baptist Church, Richmond, Virginia; Author, *Before You Open Your Bible* and *Before You Share Your Faith*

"Glen Scrivener has done us a great favour. He has taken lengthy, scholarly (and sometimes boring) history tomes and transposed their ideas into something exciting, crystal clear, and almost impossible to put down. His central thesis is that our contemporary "secular" beliefs about equality, compassion, sexual consent and even progress all ultimately derive from the Christian faith. This thesis is not so controversial in learned circles, but with a few more books like *The Air We Breathe* it may soon become common knowledge. I hope this book is very widely read. "

JOHN DICKSON, Author; Historian; Distinguished Fellow, Ridley College

"A riveting, compelling and refreshing read. Glen bottles the air of the centuries (millennia, even), distilling it into this well-researched, short, snappy read. *The Air We Breathe* is a thoughtful excavation of seven values at the heart of our society and where they came from. It sparkles with Glen's characteristically poetic storytelling, while incisively capturing abstract concepts and grounding them in historical and contemporary cultural examples. I enjoyed reading this book, and I look forward to sharing it with others."

KRISTI MAIR, Author; Speaker; Academic

"We long for justice, freedom, and equality. We believe that each and every human being—no matter how rich or poor, powerful or weak—deserves fairness, dignity and respect. But where does this vision come from? Why are we so zealous for it? What if our values aren't as self-evident as we think they are? This is why Glen Scrivener's *The Air We Breathe* is a must-read for anyone who benefits from being WEIRD (Western, Educated, Industrialised, Rich, Democratic). This book will give us the basis for our shared vision. It will give us the story behind our values. By reading this book, we will humbly acknowledge the Composer from whose songsheet we're singing."

SAM CHAN, Third Space, thirdspace.org.au

"This is such a well-written, captivating book; I could barely put it down. Glen shows us that human rights, equality and justice have been ludicrous and offensive notions for most of history. These notions hold sway today only because the Christian worldview won. Don't believe it? Read the book."

TIM FARRON, Member of Parliament, Westmorland and Lonsdale

"We are so accustomed to both Christianity and the criticisms of Christianity that we often forget the great blessings the Christian religion has brought to the world. Whether you need to be reminded of these gifts or to unwrap them for the first time, this book will challenge, encourage and enlighten you."

KAREN SWALLOW PRIOR, Research Professor of English and Christianity and Culture, Southeastern Baptist Theological Seminary; Author, *On Reading Well: Finding the Good Life through Great Books*

"Here is a fascinating, persuasive and urgently needed book. Glen presents the Christian cultural legacy as not only positive but so deeply ingrained in us that, without realising it, we often use it to attack what we dislike about 'Christianity'. Glen also shows, by implication, what we stand to lose by Christianity's erosion. Typically, however, he brings our attention back to the 'author and perfecter', Jesus Christ, asserting the simple (and maybe hard-to-face) conclusion that so much of what we know and love comes from him!"

JOEL VIRGO, Senior Pastor, Emmanuel Church, Brighton, UK

"Before the pandemic, like almost everyone else in London, I read Yuval Harari's *Sapiens*. I was troubled by his cynical story of where we come from; even with my background in neuroscience, I found the reductionism unpersuasive. Glen Scrivener argues that our modern culture, and most of the values we hold dear, originated somewhere else entirely. Love him or hate him, the teachings of Jesus Christ have infused *The Air We Breathe* more than we know. A brilliant book."

DR ANDREW SACH, Pastor; Writer

"*The Air We Breathe* is the book we need right now. In it, Scrivener provides a compelling, well-researched and confident account of the West's debt to Christianity and to Christ. The writing is full of energy and warmth. And, despite the academic rigour, the book's tone is more that of an animated argument late at night in a pub: all friendly like, but with no holds barred. I'd put this into the hands of any of my secular friends in a heartbeat."

RORY SHINER, Pastor; Author

"Dickens' classic novel *Great Expectations* turns on the moment when its hero, Pip finds out that the criminal, Magwitch, had been his sole benefactor—a man whom he'd always thought of as just a convict was actually his patron! He had despised and dismissed the man, who had in fact given him a life. This book will provide a similar turning point for many. In a riveting sweep through culture, modern and ancient history, theology and philosophy, Glen Scrivener reveals a Christian inheritance which, to our great shame, we have also despised and dismissed. Even for me as a pastor, I found it caused a paradigm shift in terms of such values as equality and compassion, freedom and progress. A must-read if we want to crack the code of what's going on in our culture."

RICO TICE, Founder, Christianity Explored Ministries

"Fascinating and eye-opening, this is a book full of insight for our time. And more: it comes bursting with hope. Wonderful stuff!"

MICHAEL REEVES, President, Union School of Theology

HOW

WE ALL

CAME TO

BELIEVE IN

THE AIR WE BREATHE

FREEDOM,

KINDNESS,

PROGRESS,

AND

EQUALITY

·

GLEN

SCRIVENER

The Air We Breathe
© 2022 Glen Scrivener. Reprinted 2022, 2023 (twice).

Published by:
The Good Book Company

thegoodbook.com | thegoodbook.co.uk
thegoodbook.com.au | thegoodbook.co.nz | thegoodbook.co.in

Cover design by Faceout Studio
Art direction and design by André Parker

ISBN: 9781784987497 | Printed in Turkey

To Julius —
now and for ever our JJ

CONTENTS

Introduction   11

1. The Night Before Christmas   23

2. Equality   41

3. Compassion   61

4. Consent   81

5. Enlightenment   101

6. Science   127

7. Freedom   149

8. Progress   167

9. The Kingdom without the King   187

10. Choose Your Miracle   205

Final Words   221

INTRODUCTION

An older goldfish swishes past a couple of small fry.
"How's the water, boys?" he enquires.
"Water?" they ask. "What's water?"

Goldfish don't see water. Goldfish see what's in the water, they see what's refracted through the water, but I assume (yes, assume—I haven't done the proper investigations) that goldfish don't see the water itself. And yet there it is. It's their environment. Universal but invisible. It shapes everything they do and everything they see. But they don't see *it*.

Here's the contention of this book: if you're a Westerner— whether you've stepped foot inside a church or not, whether you've clapped eyes on a Bible or not, whether you consider yourself an atheist, pagan or Jedi Knight— you are a goldfish, and Christianity is the water in which you swim.

Or, to say the same thing in a slightly different way, Christianity is the air we breathe. It is our atmosphere. It's our environment, both unseen and all-pervasive. And in the tradition of a spiritual teacher (truth be told, I'm an Anglican clergyman, so the shoe fits), I'm going to ask you to *focus on your breathing*. This is a technique common to so many of the great religious traditions.

The spiritual teacher does not invite you to start breathing. You've got that life skill down pat—20,000 breaths a day; you're a natural! But there's something centring about noticing your breathing. Are you doing it now? Suddenly you're slowed down. You're aware of your dependence. You're inhabiting your body as a creature with needs and rhythms and physicality. You are mindful of your connection to the world around you and your place within it.

This book is like that practice. But instead of oxygen, I'm talking about beliefs and intuitions. What I want you to do is notice your dependence on the environment around you and your place within the world of ideas. Here's a chance to slow down and pay attention to the profoundly Christian atmosphere you inhabit.

"Christian?" you say. "I'm not sure my world is particularly *Christian*." This book is, in large part, about making that case. You can be the judge of how successful it is, but here's my contention: we depend on values and goals— and ways of thinking about values and goals—that have been deeply and distinctively shaped by the Jesus-revolution (otherwise known as "Christianity"). These values are now so all-pervasive that we consider them to be universal, obvious and natural: the air we breathe.

Over the next ten chapters we will pay attention to what, ordinarily, we take for granted. I hope it will be a useful exercise for everyone, no matter how you identify religiously. Here's what you might stand to gain from it, depending on where you're coming from.

THE VIEW FROM THE OUTSIDE: THE "NONES"

The "nones" are a growing segment of Western society—those who, when asked on a survey for their religion, reply, "None". Perhaps that's you. You say, "Christianity? Remind me?" You're unfamiliar with Christian teachings, but you're interested enough to open up this book and have a look in. As you do so, you might consider yourself a total outsider to Christian faith. My first word is: don't be so sure. Goldfish might not know the chemical composition of H_2O, but it's still central to their lives. In the same way, I'm guessing that the concerns of the following chapters resonate with you: equality, compassion, consent, enlightenment, science, freedom and progress. None of these values are self-evident, nor are they widespread among the civilisations of the world. So where did they come from, and how did they get to become "the air we breathe"?

We can answer that question in one word, in two sentences or in ten chapters. The one-word answer is: Christianity. The two-sentence answer goes something like this:

> *The extraordinary impact of Christianity is seen in the fact that you don't notice it. You already hold particularly "Christian-ish" views, and the fact that you think of these values as natural, obvious or universal shows how profoundly the Christian revolution has shaped you.*

If the two-sentence summary strikes you as novel, bizarre, stupid or offensive, that's ok. I don't expect instant agreement. I've got a lot of work ahead of me— hence the need for the ten chapters. But, if you're game,

I'd like to take you on a journey from the ancient world to the modern and from the beginning of the Bible to the end of history. I hope that along the way we'll have some fun, that you'll get a deeper appreciation for the values you cherish, and, most of all, that you'll see the power and profundity of Jesus and his revolution. In the meantime, let me turn to a different kind of objection.

THE VIEW FROM BEYOND: THE "DONES"

Perhaps you *are* familiar with Christianity, but you've rejected it. You object to the idea that Christianity is the air you breathe. You say, "Been there, done that. 13 years at a church school. No thanks!" Or you say, "I studied Christianity at this point or other". Or, "I was a regular churchgoer, but it's no longer for me". I take all of those experiences seriously. I can also respect the reasons why you might feel that the Christian faith is not for you. Nevertheless, I don't think you're done with Christianity, any more than you're done with breathing. It's not the sort of thing you point to, *over there, back then*. Like air, Christianity is so pervasive that we cannot help depending on it, even as we protest against it.

We might feel that Christianity is unequal, cruel, coercive, ignorant, anti-science, restrictive or backwards. That is, in fact, a pretty common list of objections to the Christian faith, and, at points, the shoe fits. But I didn't pick those seven objections at random. I simply reversed the seven core values at the heart of this book. The reason why those seven accusations bite is because, deep down, we believe in the seven values. Our problems with Christianity (and we all have problems with it, especially Christians!) turn out to be *Christian* problems.

So then, if you feel yourself to be "done" with Christianity, my desire is to take your critiques more seriously, not less. I want you to embrace those difficulties and press into them since, in truly owning those standards, you may well find yourself coming closer to the essence of Christian faith. At the end of the book I hope to show you some positive steps forward, not as a way of diminishing or dismissing your critiques but as a way of grounding them.

There's a third kind of reader I'm interested in.

THE VIEW FROM WITHIN: THE "WONS"

Perhaps you are a Christian, and you're looking out at a particularly fractious world. You're wondering how we got here, where we're heading and whether your faith— so ancient in its origins—can make sense of it all today. I want to encourage you to see that what we're witnessing in the world are the ongoing convulsions of the Jesus revolution—a revolution predicted, proclaimed and propelled from the depths of history and experienced in the details of the everyday. In tracing the development of this revolution, I hope you'll be strengthened in faith and encouraged to share it. Jesus Christ is not a peripheral concern for a few spiritual hobbyists. He's the Lord of history, and in him our lives, our beliefs, our practices and our world make sense.

WHAT YOU WILL FIND

Here's the journey I want to take you on. First, I want to show you that the air we breathe is peculiar. To do that we'll have to leave our familiar environs. I had no idea how sweetly Australia smelt until I left. The eucalyptus trees perfume the atmosphere, but I'd never noticed it until I'd spent years away from home. Now when I fly back to Sydney, it's the warm, sweet air that hits me first. In the next chapter I want to take us out of the familiar and place us in the ancient world—a world untouched by Christianity. We will notice the profound differences in culture, assumptions, beliefs, intuitions and ideals. Any notion that our modern, liberal views are obvious, natural or universal must contend with the profoundly alien views taken by the rest of the world and the rest of history. As the writer L.P. Hartley put it, "The past is a foreign country: they do things differently there".

Next, we will sketch out some major landmarks in the development of the Christian story as we explore seven values that are central to the modern outlook:

Equality: *We believe in the equal moral status of every member of the human family, no matter their rank, race, religion, gender or sexuality.*

Compassion: *We believe a society should be judged by the way it treats its weakest members.*

Consent: *We believe that the powerful have no right to force themselves on others.*

Enlightenment: *We believe in education for all and its power to transform a society.*

Science: *We believe in science: its ability to help us understand the world and improve our lives.*

Freedom: *We believe that persons are not property and that each of us should be in control of our own lives.*

Progress: *We believe in moral improvement over time and that we should continue to reform society of its former evils.*

The heart of the book comprises these seven chapters. Roughly speaking, we'll be moving from the beginning of the Bible through to today as the chapters progress: from Genesis to George Floyd. The equality chapter introduces teaching from the start of the Bible (the Old Testament). The compassion chapter explores the arrival of Jesus of Nazareth (the New Testament). The consent chapter follows the early church and its moral revolution. The enlightenment chapter sketches some developments between the fall of Rome (410) and the Protestant Reformation of the 16th century. The science chapter spends much of its time with the founders of the modern scientific method (in the 16th and 17th century). The freedom chapter explores the abolition of the trans-Atlantic slave trade and its aftermath (the 18th and 19th centuries). Finally, in the progress chapter, we look at the 20th century—at its moral monsters, like Hitler, and its moral heroes, like Martin Luther King.

WHAT YOU WON'T FIND

You might notice from the sketch above that my telling of the story is very Western focused. This is emphatically not because "West is best". It's not. As we travel along, we will witness some horrendous evils. Even the "successes" are mixed, to say the least. We should also be aware that Christian history is far more global than our telling of it here. Long before European Christianity was a force in the world, the faith had spread south (Ethiopia was one of the world's first Christian countries) and east (the Byzantine Empire was a 1,000-year Christianised civilisation which, in many ways, outshone its "younger brother" in the West).

Today, Christianity is the most diverse sociological phenomenon the world has ever seen. About a quarter of Christians live in Central or South America, a quarter in Africa and a quarter in Europe, and the last quarter is fairly evenly split between North America and Asia. What's more, its make-up is set to continue a shift southwards and eastwards. For instance, the rate of Christian growth in China has been estimated at 10% per annum for the last 40 years. If that rate continues, there will be more Christians in China than in the United States by the year 2030. Christianity is *not* a Western phenomenon.[1]

Why then the Western focus in this book? Two reasons. Firstly, the West has undoubtedly had an immense global impact, for better and for worse (and don't worry—we will look at the worse too). For instance, in my own branch of Christianity, I am part of the worldwide Anglican "communion" (the third largest grouping of churches in the world). All such churches trace their roots

---

1 "As of 2010, about a quarter of the global Christian population was in Europe (26%), a quarter in Latin America and the Caribbean (25%) and a quarter in sub-Saharan Africa (24%). Significant numbers of Christians also live in Asia and the Pacific (13%) and North America (12%)." The Pew Research Center: *The Future of World Religions: Population Growth Projections, 2010-2050.* https://www.pewforum.org/2015/04/02/christians/. Accessed 25th October 2021. See also Antonia Blumberg, "China on Track to Become World's Largest Christian Country by 2025, Experts Say," Huffpost, 22nd April 2014, http://www.huffingtonpost.com/2014/04/22/china-largest-christiancountry_n_5191910.html. Accessed 25th October 2021.

back to the Church of England and its distinctive history, and yet the average Anglican in the world today is a black, teenage girl from Nigeria.[2] (Nigeria, by the way, contains more Anglicans than Britain has people.) I, growing up in far-flung Australia, and that Nigerian teenager, growing up in Lagos, share a spiritual family tree with roots all the way around the world. To explore Western history is not to ignore global history but to inform it.

The second reason this book has a Western focus is because I'm writing largely to an English-speaking audience (mostly in the UK, the US and Australia). I'm writing about the air I breathe, and I'm assuming it's the kind of air you breathe too. Other atmospheres are available, but if we're going to "focus on our breathing", then we need to begin where we are.

Something else you might notice from the shape of the book is its uneven timeline. Some chapters have a millennium or more to cover, others zero in on a century. That's because my central concern is to communicate the seven values more than to follow a chronology. My background is in philosophy and theology. I'm more of an "ideas" person, and this is a relatively short book. For those wanting to delve deeper, let me suggest some serious works of scholarship that have helped my own understanding:

- For more on equality: *Inventing the Individual* by Larry Siedentop

---

2 *Communities of Faith in Africa and the African Diaspora*, ed. Casely B. Essamuah and David K Ngaruiya (Pickwick Publications, 2014), p 321.

- For more on compassion: *Destroyer of the gods*
  by Larry Hurtado
- For more on consent: *From Shame to Sin*
  by Kyle Harper
- For more on enlightenment: *The Light Ages*
  by Seb Falk
- For more on science: *The Warfare between Science
  and Religion: The Idea That Wouldn't Die*, edited by
  Jeff Hardin
- For more on freedom: *In the Image of God*
  by David Brion Davis
- For more on progress: *Protestants* by Alec Ryrie

To get the larger historical sweep, I recommend, among
other books:

- *Dominion* by Tom Holland
- *Atheist Delusions* by D.B. Hart
- *The Book That Made Your World*
  by Vishal Mangalwadi
- *The Triumph of Christianity* by Rodney Stark
- *Bullies and Saints* by John Dickson
- *The WEIRDest People in the World*
  by Joseph Henrich

Such historians, scientists and sociologists, whether
Christian or not (mostly they're not), reach the same
arresting conclusion: our modern, Western values are
W.E.I.R.D. Joseph Henrich, one of the authors above,
coined the acronym along with other social scientists
to describe the peculiarity of our modern assumptions.
Our distinctive outlook in the West is a minority report
in world history. It has emerged in cultures that are

Western, Educated, Industrialised, Rich and Democratic. What Henrich (and the others listed above) go on to say is that it's Christianity that has made the difference. Unmistakably the WEIRD West has its roots in the Jesus revolution.

At the end of the book there are two chapters reflecting on the implications of all this. Chapter 9 will discuss the position in which the West finds itself. Chapter 10 considers the ways the Bible has charted this course in advance; and then, finally, I draw out some lessons for the "nones", the "dones" and the "wons" alike.

But first, we begin by visiting that strange country called the past. Let's explore the thoughts and attitudes of the ancient world before the advent of Christianity. From a believer's point of view, there was a long night before Christmas.

1. THE NIGHT BEFORE CHRISTMAS

"Well, that's Western art for you. A thousand years of crucifixions,
then stripes."

— A visitor to the National Gallery, London,
as reported on Twitter, 2017[3]

"A thousand years of crucifixions, then stripes." As a summary of the history of Western art, it goes without saying that this statement is ridiculously reductionistic (did I mention this was on Twitter?). But still... have you been to the National Gallery? If you were to whizz through its Western Art section and then write a tweet-length summary, you might struggle to improve on this quote.

Behind the humour, the quip gets at something remarkable: Jesus Christ, and especially his gruesome death, has towered above Western civilization. The cross is the most globally recognised symbol, certainly of religion, but perhaps of anything.

This fact is remarkable not just for the scale of the impact but for the event that is being commemorated. An outsider

---

3 https://twitter.com/sannewman/status/874624753092489216?s=20. Accessed 2nd
   November 2021.

to Christianity and its art might expect depictions of Christ's birth to predominate, or his baptism, or anything really—anything other than his violent death. The idea of presenting a tortured man as art is subversive to say the least. To claim—as Christians do—that the man on the cross was *God* is the most revolutionary notion the world has ever entertained.

One of the signs that we are children of this particular revolution is the fact that we can stroll through the climate-controlled corridors of a gallery and, upon entering the religious wing, proceed to nod sagely at dozens of depictions of death by torture. "Ah, sacred art!" we sigh. For the most part this incongruity goes unnoticed. Yet this only proves the immense impact of the Jesus movement. The way we see the cross has been revolutionised because the cross has revolutionised the way we see.

To make my point, let me contrast the "sacred art" of the National Gallery with a much older portrayal of the cross. The earliest surviving depiction of Christ's crucifixion is a piece of graffiti mocking the strange new cult called Christianity. It was found scratched into the plaster of a wall on Rome's Palatine Hill. The graffiti shows a figure on a cross with the body of a man and the head of a donkey. Standing by the cross is a devotee with his hand raised in veneration. The caption says it all: "Alexamenos worships his god".

Comedy doesn't always hold up over time, but the mockery here hits its mark today just as powerfully as it would have done 2,000 years ago. The message is clear:

a man on a cross is not a God; he's an ass. Anyone who venerates such a figure is a fool at best and probably perverse.

It's worth asking ourselves the question: who sees the cross more clearly—the Roman mocker or the sacred artist? As we press into this topic, we will consider that we are the weird ones. In this chapter we will step into the sandals of the Romans, to see the world as they saw it. No Roman would show a casual appreciation of crucifixion. Their reaction would be as different to ours as night is to day. If the coming of Christ has been a new dawn (Christians certainly think so), then this chapter explores the nighttime before that first Christmas.

THE SLAVE'S DEATH

"Wretched is the loss of one's good name in the public courts, wretched, too, a monetary fine exacted from one's property, and wretched is exile ... But the executioner, the veiling of heads, and the very word 'cross,' let them all be far removed from not only the bodies of Roman citizens but even from their thoughts, their eyes, and their ears ... the mere mention of them [is] unworthy of a Roman citizen and a free man."[4]

So said Cicero (106–43 BC), one of history's greatest orators. Notice here the concern for honour and the disdain of shame. Worthiness and wretchedness were

---

4 M. Tullius Cicero, *Speech before Roman Citizens on Behalf of Gaius Rabirius, Defendant Against the Charge of Treason*, ed. William Blake Tyrrell. http://www.perseus.tufts.edu/hopper/text?doc=Perseus%3Atext%3A1999.02.0023%3Achapter%3D5%3Asection%3D16. Accessed 28th October 2021.

the heaven and hell of the ancient world. To Cicero and his peers, "one's good name", one's citizenship, one's free status were paramount. To lose them was to lose everything. No wonder, then, that the very mention of the cross was a horror to Cicero. Crucifixion was of course extremely painful. (We get our word "excruciating" from the Latin *ex crucis*: "from the cross".) Yet, more than this, it was humiliating. To be impaled, naked, before the watching world was as undignified an end as the Romans could devise. And the shame was a large part of the point.

To us, the cross has become a sacred symbol and, as such, embodies the very opposite of its ancient meaning. Even if we're not religious ourselves, we might understand the cross to be a symbol of redemption, salvation, God's presence even among the lowly, and God's peace even amid our pain. In the ancient world it meant the reverse. It symbolised degradation, worthlessness, unremitting torture and unredeemed loss—"the extreme penalty", according to Roman historian Tacitus.[5] Corpses cut down from the cross would routinely be cast into a ditch to be pecked at by birds and eaten by dogs. Those crucified were garbage.

The cross was "the slave's punishment".[6] Roman society, as with every ancient culture, was arranged as a vertiginously steep hierarchy. That hierarchy was not simply one of rank or role; it was a hierarchy of *being*. The punishments of the state were an expression—and an

5   Tacitus, Historiae 4.11.

6   Tacitus, Annals 15.44.

enforcement—of this hierarchy. Certain classes of people could not be crucified and certain classes could.

Cicero called crucifixion "the most miserable and most painful punishment, appropriate to slaves alone".[7] While it was proper to crucify slaves, Cicero went on to discuss the horrors of an incident when a Roman citizen had been mistakenly crucified. "It is a crime to bind a Roman citizen; to scourge him is a wickedness; to put him to death is almost parricide [killing a parent]. What shall I say of crucifying him? So guilty an action cannot by any possibility be adequately expressed by any name bad enough for it."[8] Crucifixion was either "appropriate" or an unspeakable evil, depending on who was on the cross.

In AD 61 a Roman senator was killed by one of his slaves. Custom dictated that every slave in the household—all four hundred of them—must be crucified. Some in Rome objected, said Tacitus, and "shrank from extreme rigour" in carrying out the sentence. But the majority in the Senate agreed with Cassius Caius, who spoke powerfully in favour of the mass execution. Quite obviously, to Caius, tradition was to trump any feelings of pity. He asked, "Is it your pleasure to search for arguments in a matter already weighed in the deliberations of wiser men than ourselves?" The ancients had spoken; who were moderns to object? (You will notice this is the very

---

7   M. Tullius Cicero, *Against Verres*, ed. C.D. Yonge. http://www.perseus.tufts.edu/hopper/text?doc=Perseus%3Atext%3A1999.02.0018%3Atext%3DVer.%3Aactio%3D2%3Abook%3D5%3Asection%3D169. Accessed 29th October 2021.

8   As above. http://www.perseus.tufts.edu/hopper/text?doc=Perseus%3Atext%3A1999.02.0018%3Atext%3DVer.%3Aactio%3D2%3Abook%3D5%3Asection%3D170. Accessed 2nd November 2021.

opposite of today's belief in progress.) Against those who worried that some innocents may die, Caius argued, "There is some injustice in every great precedent, which, though injurious to individuals, has its compensation in the public advantage". Here is an argument for "the greater good", where individuals are sacrificed to the public advantage. Why? To set a precedent. To make an example. "It is only by terror you can hold in such a motley rabble." It was only terror that maintained the caste system of Rome. Only by terror could the few nobles "live singly amid numbers, safe among a trembling throng".[9]

Such arguments carried the day and 400 men, women and children, were dragged to 400 crosses. Thus was upheld the wisdom of the ancients, the greater good of the empire, and the terrorising of the masses. Deterrence was the goal and crucifixion a major tool. Sometimes the injustice of it all was the very point being made. To see "the slaves' punishment" inflicted publicly on, sometimes, hundreds of the unwashed masses—even innocents— was to see their worthlessness in the starkest terms. The powers that be killed *those people* because they could. And the more they butchered them, the more they felt able to butcher them. As one victim of Roman brutality said, "[our torturers were commanded] to think and act as if we no longer existed".[10] To see someone crucified was to

---

9   Tacitus, "The Murder of Pedanius Secundus". https://faculty.tnstate.edu/tcorse/ H1210revised/tacitus.html. Accessed 27th October 2021.

10 "The Writings of Phileas the Martyr describing the Occurrences at Alexandria." https://www.ccel.org/ccel/schaff/npnf201.iii.xiii.xi.html?scrBook=Phil&scrCh=2& scrV=6#highlight. Accessed 27th October 2021.

watch their un-person-ing and to hear the message, *Do not go the way of this wretch.*

This is not to say that the onlookers disliked watching. On the contrary, executions were wildly popular. Crucifixions were always public and would sometimes form part of the gladiatorial games. In Rome vast crowds would watch exquisite horrors, including crucifixions as half-time entertainment. Slaves fighting to the death was the meat and potatoes, but the spice was often provided by wild animals devouring prisoners, or perhaps even raping them and then eating them. It was even boasted at the time that the *bestiarii* (the wild-animal tamers) could train a bull to rape its victim first—or at least simulate the attack. All this was to the delight of the crowd and the honour of the gods, who took the form of beasts to rape women. These bloody re-enactments of ancient scenes—whether divine, military or bestial—were a particular favourite of the crowds.

Such inventive and grotesque brutality valued spectacle dear and life cheap. In Caligula's reign (AD 37–41), there was a time of scarcity when meat needed to feed the games' beasts became too expensive. The emperor's solution was to order all the city's prisoners, whether they'd received a trial or not, to be fed to the starving animals. In Rome some kinds of people could be pet food. In truth, these victims weren't even "people"— certainly not in a way that would be recognisable to our modern sensibilities.

Yet far from this hierarchy of value being lamented, it was lauded. It was just. This is what "Nature herself" taught.

WHAT NATURE TEACHES

"Nature herself intimates that it is just for the better to have more than the worse, the more powerful than the weaker... Justice consists in the superior ruling over and having more than the inferior."

(Plato, 428–348 BC)

"For that some should rule and others be ruled is a thing not only necessary, but expedient; from the hour of their birth, some are marked out for subjection, others for rule." (Aristotle, 384–322 BC)

The Greek philosopher Plato, together with his teacher Socrates (470–399 BC) and his student, Aristotle, are considered the fathers of Western philosophy. It's often said that the history of thought following Plato consists, basically, of footnotes to his teaching. Even the mighty Romans had to admit that when it came to *intellectual* firepower, the Greeks led the way. No Roman—indeed, no ancient—would have quibbled with the views expressed above. And yet they are the very reverse of our modern thinking. We consider "justice" to mean the equalising of persons. The classical world considered justice as the enforcement of inequality; that was what nature intended.

To Plato and Aristotle it was obvious that certain humans were born to be "living tools": machines to be used by others. The other name for this is slaves.

Often, classical writers such as Plato or Aristotle are cited as having "defended slavery". In truth, they did no such thing—because no one was attacking it. No one thought to. It wasn't just that the entire economy was built on slavery; politics and religion were too. In fact, the very fabric of being, as understood by the ancients, had slavery woven into it. As Larry Siedentop comments, "At the core of ancient thinking [was] the assumption of natural inequality".[11]

Ancient philosophers did not think of themselves as defenders or even teachers of such inequality. "Nature herself" taught that some were fitter, stronger, smarter, and, frankly, better than others. There were superior races (Greeks over barbarians), superior sexes (men over women), and superior classes (free men over slaves). The deformity and inferiority of barbarians, women and slaves was clear from their very nature. How could anyone deny that some people can govern well, while others need governing?

This much was obvious to every member of the classical world, wherever they found themselves in the hierarchy of being. Certainly, there were those who sought a change to the status quo. A revolt of the slaves was something always to be guarded against—hence the need for violent deterrents like crucifixion. But when inferiors reached for greater status, power, freedom or goods, they were seeking for advantages, not rights—for privilege, not justice. As Plato states above, justice *was* your superiors ruling over you. That was what nature decreed, and those most in tune with reason could see that. The position which fate had assigned you was simply your just deserts.

---

11   Larry Siedentop, *Inventing the Individual* (Penguin, 2015), p 51.

The wisdom of the people, distilled in teaching like Aesop's fables (7th century BC), reinforced this message. One of Aesop's tales told of a lizard who wished to be a stag, but when he saw the stag hunted and killed, he ceased from his foolish ambition. He ends the fable glad of his own ignominious spot in the food chain. Likewise, there was the lizard who wished to be long like a snake. He stretched himself out beyond his proper bounds and—stupid lizard!—burst.

These stories teach the opposite lesson to our modern tales. Nowadays the hero casts off the shackles of tradition and hierarchy to release their awesome inner potential. Perhaps that's a better lesson, perhaps not— what is undeniable is the difference. Ancient people were taught in a thousand ways to "know their place". And their place was not just their rank in society; it was their position in the cosmos—their position in the great hierarchy of being. Religion was, therefore, an integral part of their lives.

WHAT RELIGION TEACHES

In a sense, there is no need for this as a distinct section. As we discuss ancient religion, we're not really moving to another subject, at least, not as far as ancient peoples were concerned. As we'll see when we get to chapter 5, it is only as a result of the Christian revolution that we now tend to distinguish between a secular and a sacred realm. As modern people, we think of the public, tangible, everyday operations of the world—the realm of science, commerce, politics, and so on. We then contrast this with the personal, inward realm of "religion". When I think of "the secular sphere", I imagine a 1980s corporate video with upbeat synth pop music and shots of business-suited New Yorkers bustling to work. When I think "religious", I think of soft-focused church scenes, a lone choirboy singing, a lone candle, a lone pray-er. The latter is a peculiar hobby of the few; the former is what makes the world go round.

But this divide would have been alien to the ancient world. They would never have thought, for instance, to separate politics and religion. Politics concerned the affairs of the *polis*, the Greek word for city. Yet the city was an aggregation *not* of individuals, as we might understand them, but of families. At the head of each family was the father of the household (the *paterfamilias*). He was the oldest male, who held life-or-death power over every other family member. His most vital role was as priest of the family cult, to maintain worship to the family's gods, to keep the fires of the hearth burning as proper honour to their ancestors, and to hand over such sacred duties to the eldest son. When these families united into larger clans and cities, the gods were a crucial aspect of such associations. Agreements—whether commercial, military or political—were ratified by the gods and by sacred acts. To be a citizen was to share in the worship of the city's gods.

Even when Athens experimented with what it called "democracy", it was a thoroughly religious enterprise. Instead of a mon-archy (rule by one), or olig-archy (rule by a few), demo-cracy was the "power of the people". The crucial question is, of course, whom did the Greeks consider to be "the people"? When we consider "the people", we might think of a group of individuals who stand equally under the same law. But that's our Christianity coming through. Instead, the fundamental unit for the ancient world (and for much of the non-Christian world today) was the family. When these family units united, it was the "fathers" who came together. Under "democracy" these priestly heads of households were able to vote on a range of matters or candidates, but their options had already been limited by casting lots or consulting, say, the Delphic Oracle. It was divination more than democracy that ruled Athens. So while, at points, a minority of elite males may have had the vote, it was the gods who called the shots. Everything—from the rule of the city to the outcome of wars, to the success of the crops, to the study of the heavenly spheres—was "religious" to the core.

Therefore, to understand ancient people, we need to understand their religious thinking. Let's do that now by outlining some of their origins stories. The creation myths of old give a vivid impression of the way people saw the gods, themselves and the world around them.

BORN TO SLAVE
In the beginning there was chaos. Then rebellion. Then war. Then slavery. Then us. So said the myths of the ancient Near East.

The Babylonian creation story serves as a typical tale. In the *Enuma Elish*, most of the story concerns the battles of the gods prior to creation. Eventually it is Marduk who slays Tiamat, whose body is split into sky and land (heaven and earth). 300 of the gods are assigned to the sky and 600 to the land, and humanity is made by the sacrifice of a god so that "the toil of the gods will be laid" on humans. "From [Kingu's] blood [Ea] created mankind, on whom he imposed the service of the gods, [to] set the gods free."[12]

This is a recurring theme in the ancient myths. Humanity is made from bloodshed and formed for slavery. Compare the Mesopotamian *Atrahasis* myth, where it says, "Create primeval man, that he may bear the yoke! Let him bear the yoke ... Let man bear the load of the gods!"[13] Yet again humanity is made by sacrificing a god (this time the unfortunate deity is Geshtu-E), and yet again humanity is pressed into hard labour.

According to the Greek myths, our origins involve chaos, warfare and slavery—yes—but also plenty of jealousy and sex too. The Greeks spoke of Gaia (earth), Ouranos (heaven/sky), and Tartaros (the underworld). Gaia and Ouranos have children: Titans. But Gaia also gives birth to monsters—cyclops—who disgust Ouranos. He hurls them into Tartaros. Gaia decides to take revenge by getting one of her sons, Kronos, to chop off Ouranos's genitals. In an unexpected silver lining to this marital feud, the blood of his genitals creates Aphrodite, goddess of love and beauty. Just when you thought romance was dead.

Kronos marries his sister Rhea but then fears that his children will cut him up, so, in a pre-emptive strike,

12 Enuma Elish, 29-34. http://www.usu.edu/markdamen/ANE/lectures/10.1.pdf. Accessed 29th October 2021.

13 Atrahasis, Tablet 1. https://geha.paginas.ufsc.br/files/2017/04/Atrahasis.pdf. Accessed 29th October 2021.

he swallows them as soon as they're each born. Rhea manages to save her sixth-born, Zeus, who grows up, nurtured by a goat in a Cretan cave. He returns to trick Kronos into vomiting up his other children. Zeus then forges an alliance with his regurgitated sibling gods. They are the Olympians, and they fight the Titans. Long story short, the Olympians win, and Zeus cuts up Kronos (just as Kronos had feared), throwing the pieces into Tartaros. Zeus becomes king of the gods with Poseidon ruling over the seas and Hades ruling the underworld.

Where does humanity fit in? For our existence, we have Prometheus to thank. Prometheus was a Titan, but he was not thrown into Tartaros with his fellow Titans because he had not fought in the war. Together with others, Prometheus is tasked with making humans. He forges man from the dust; Athena breathes life into him, but, for the crowning touch, Prometheus, against Zeus's wishes, steals fire from the sun and gives it to man. (Titans love humans more than Olympians do.) For this rebellious act, Prometheus is chained to a rock and has his liver eaten by an eagle, and then regrown, and then eaten again, and then regrown. And then... You get the idea.

These are our origins: chaos, violence, and death. And this is the case wherever we turn in the ancient world. The Romans adopted much of the Greek mythology, performing more of a rebrand than a rewrite. Zeus was now "Jupiter", Aphrodite was "Venus", Poseidon was "Neptune"; but the stories contained the same themes of jealousies, intrigues and brutality. One significant update was the Roman take on Ares, the Greek god of war. Where the Greeks considered Ares to be a destructive and contemptible force, the Romans loved their version, Mars. He was the very picture of virility, second only to Jupiter in the pantheon. He fathered the founders of Rome— Romulus and Remus—by his rape of the unsuspecting mortal Rhea Silvia. When considering the origins stories of Roman mythology, it's fair to say that the city itself was the focus. The Romans' vision for the cosmos was very much centred on Rome, the "Eternal City". And that city was born of war and rape.

PROPPING UP THE COSMOS

In this chapter we have been attempting to stand in the sandals of a Roman. In particular we want to see the cross in the way they saw it. It's nearly impossible to do this since our WEIRD values get in the way. As we hear of rape and violence, inequality and brutality, slavery and death-by-torture, our modern sensibilities kick in. We find it hard to accept these as "the way things are". We certainly find it difficult to consider them as "the way things *should be*". But a Roman took all of this in their stride. And as they stood at the foot of a cross, they had a gutter-level view of the whole terrifying structure of reality that towered above. The cross came down from violent powers on high to crush the contemptible and maintain the "just" order of the empire—in fact, of the cosmos. To look upon a victim of crucifixion was to see a man at rock bottom.

And then Christians came along and said, "We see something else". Their claim was the most revolutionary imaginable: that God himself had hung on a cross. Not Mars, obviously. When Mars came in peace, he sheathed his spear as a sign of his magnanimity. The Christian

God did not sheath his spear. Quite the opposite: he had one plunged into his heart by a Roman soldier as he died the death of a slave. And the first people to call this figure "God" were the last people you would expect. Christianity began as a Jewish movement. All Christ's earliest followers were Jews. And they all called him God. When a Jew said "God", they did not mean a member of the Greek or Roman pantheon, and they did not mean a squabbling deity from the Babylonian myths. They meant "the Maker of heaven and earth, the Source of life and being". And yet, in the first instance, it was Jews who became Christians, and they did so by looking to a crucified man and declaring, "Behold our God"!

What would a Roman—breathing Roman air, kept in check by Roman brutalities, raised on Roman myths— make of the Christian claim? They would, of course, consider Christ an ass, his worshippers fools and his religion a perversity. If Roman citizens could not bear to have the name of the cross on their lips, what sort of God would show up as its victim?

"The message of the cross is foolishness," admitted Paul, a 1st-century Jew-turned-Christian who spent decades preaching this message around the Mediterranean. "But," he added, "to us who are being saved it is the power of God" (1 Corinthians 1:18).[14] Paul went on to write half the New Testament, and he summarised his basic message as an obsession with "Christ and him crucified" (2:2). He presented the crucifixion of Jesus as a stark

---

14 That is, the Bible book of 1 Corinthians, chapter 1, verse 18. Subsequent references to the Bible follow this same format.

dividing line, with some deriding it and some devoted to it. Naturally speaking, a 1st-century hearer could only find it stupid, and a particularly shameful kind of stupid too. "God on a cross" was painfully imbecilic as an idea. And yet for Christians, something about it made sense—it made sense of their lives and their world. They felt themselves to have been met by the God of heaven, who had deigned to stoop. For them, rock bottom became ground zero. The cross was the epicentre of an earthquake whose reverberations shook every earthly certainty. The Highest had plumbed the lowest depths and begun a radical movement to upend the world.

Paul and his other 1st-century contemporaries persisted with their foolish preaching, and, remarkably, they gained a hearing. Over time their belief that Christ crucified was also "the power of God" began to look less and less ridiculous because a power seemed to be at work. A movement was beginning. First minds changed, then lives, then communities, then cultures, then everything. Eventually this foolish message became the most influential in human history.

Now the idea of humble sacrifice has gone from shameful to glorious. Now we consider equality, compassion, freedom and all the WEIRD values this book explores as obvious. Now we wander blithely through galleries to gaze upon "a thousand years of crucifixions". Whatever moral earthquake occurred, its impact has been seismic. The rest of this book will examine it.

2. EQUALITY

"I don't accept that all lives are of equal value."

— Lord Sumption, January 2021

The outrage provoked by these words was immediate, visceral, and very Christian.

The statement belongs to Lord Sumption, former UK Supreme Court Justice. He was on TV, debating whether the government-mandated lockdown was a proportionate response to the pandemic.[15] He reasoned that, while the elderly were more affected by COVID, the young were more affected by lockdown. Therefore lockdown had been "punishing too many for the greater good".

This of course prompted the question: *if you do not lock down, are the elderly to be sacrificed for the good of the young?*

Speaking as a retiree, Sumption seemed prepared to make that sacrifice. "My children's and my grandchildren's lives are worth much more than mine because they've got a lot more of it ahead." This was the context in which he said, "I don't accept that all lives are of equal value."

In speaking of human "value" and "worth" as unequal, Sumption triggered an outrage that filled the column

---

15   *The Big Questions*, BBC1, Series 14, Episode 1. Aired 17th January 2021.

inches of the newspapers and the daytime TV slots for the next week. It did not help his cause that, within minutes of questioning our equal human value, Sumption was confronted on-air by Deborah James, a woman vulnerable to COVID due to her cancer. She protested, "With all due respect, I am the person who you say their life is not valuable". Sumption interrupted her with a clarification that injected a cubic ton of cortisol into the news cycle for the next seven days: "I didn't say your life was not valuable; I said it was less valuable".

Not worthless. Just worth less. To the surprise of no one, this clarification did not pour oil on troubled waters. It's difficult to think of a statement more likely to offend our deepest moral sensibilities. The idea that the young are more valuable than the old or that the healthy are more valuable than the sick stirs in us an indignation that is, well, religious. No other kind of language seems fit for purpose. Sumption, we feel, is blaspheming. Or something close to it. Deborah James spoke for many in her comeback to the retired judge:

> "Who are you to put a value on life? In my view, and I think in many others', life is sacred, and I don't think we should make those judgment calls. All life is worth saving regardless of what life it is people are living."

Notice the instinctive revulsion at the idea of inequality. Those who might never use the word "sacred" in any other setting begin reaching for it. When we fear that the value of equal human worth is under threat, we can't help but move our language to a religious register. To deny it is sacrilegious. It is a transgression. It's blasphemy.

"EQUALITY" AND "GOD": MATTERS OF FAITH

Imagine there's another guest on the TV show. Plato is brought in, blinking at the studio lights and baffled by the technology. He's asked whether he agrees with the claim: "Some lives are worth more than others". The ancient thinker frowns: *what is the debate exactly?*

It is trivially obvious to the father of Western philosophy that lives are of unequal value. Some are men, and some are women; some are Greeks, and some are barbarians; some are free, and some are slaves. There are rich and poor, wise and foolish, strong and weak. All that we see in nature is difference. Compare any two people concerning any one attribute and what will you conclude? This one has more than that one. This, of course, is the definition of unequal. To insist that two people are equal really, when every human trait betrays inequality, raises the question: *Equal how? Where is this magical realm where their "equality" exists? Can you show it to me?* If Plato was being polite, he might say, "Your faith in 'equality' fascinates me, and I'd like to be able to see what you see. Clearly 'equality' is very important to you. You live your life in the light of this belief, and I can respect that. But to me it looks as if you've just decided to believe in something with no reason or evidence. I'm afraid I'm not convinced."

This is how Plato might view our modern belief in "equality". Interestingly, it's exactly how my atheist friends consider God: a nice idea with no reason to believe in it. We'll press into the similarities between belief in "equality" and belief in "God" shortly. But let's return to Sumption for a minute.

THE VERTICAL AND THE HORIZONTAL

Later in the week, Sumption tried again to explain himself, this time on a different TV channel.[16] It began much better for him:

> *"I was making a perfectly simple point. Every policy-maker has got to make difficult choices. Sometimes that involves putting a value on human life. It's a standard concept in health economics: quality-adjusted life years. That's what I was talking about. Policy-makers have to do that; otherwise they cannot weigh up the consequences of different policy choices."*

This is true. In a world of scarce resources we simply cannot afford every life-saving measure. Spending money on one treatment takes money away from others, and we do not have infinite money. Therefore, in the interests of valuing life—valuing as much of it as we can—policy-makers will sometimes consider the amount of life a patient or a population has ahead of them. If we have a 9-year-old and a 99-year-old and we can only afford one life-saving treatment, Sumption says *we know what to do*. But crucially, at this point, he added a perspective which he did not articulate earlier:

> *"It doesn't mean that people are morally worth less; it doesn't mean they're worth less in the eyes of God or in the eyes of their fellow citizens..."*

Here is the vital dimension missing from Sumption's earlier comments: the vertical. There is a moral equality

---

16 *Good Morning Britain*, ITV1, Aired 18th January 2021. https://www.itv.com/goodmorningbritain/articles/lord-sumption-expands-on-his-cancer-patients-lives-are-less-valuable. Accessed 1st November 2021.

of all people—they are equal before God, equal as citizens before the same law, regardless of age, health or wealth, with no one left out. This is the kind of sentiment which resonates with us (though many would be happier if we kept the "God" bit out of it). Yet immediately Sumption returned to the horizontal dimension and to his earlier phrasing:

> "But sometimes policy-makers have to say, 'Some lives are worth more than others...'"

With the mention of "lives ... worth more", the studio erupted as before. This was heresy, and Sumption's careful explanations—whatever their merits—were lost in the howls.

My interest is not in Sumption's reasoning. His arguments, when taken in context and with caveats, were far better than his articulation of them. But given our modern beliefs and instincts, his words could only ever trigger an instinctual horror. And so they did.

In this chapter I want us to listen to that horror. Such horror rises up within us from particularly Christian places.

MODERN ORIGIN STORIES

Yuval Noah Harari has written a number of runaway bestsellers, most notably *Sapiens* and *Homo Deus*. As a historian, he is convinced that we cannot properly face the future if we do not understand our past. Yet our past, as he is at pains to point out, is a terrifying world of struggle. Just as the ancients saw our world emerging from warfare and death, Harari places us in an evolutionary story that is no less disturbing. *Homo sapiens* has come to dominate the planet through a violence, greed and pride that could equal that of any Olympian. We are by no means the fastest, nor strongest, nor toughest species on the planet, yet somehow we have become its undisputed rulers.

So what has been the secret of our success? Harari says we dominate because we co-operate—flexibly and at scale. Put one of us on a desert island and it's unlikely we'll survive. Put a family or a clan of us there and we will soon make it our own. Why do we co-operate so well? Because we tell stories. Such storytelling is not a hobby for us—it's where we find meaning. We put ourselves into these stories, identifying with certain characters and goals, and these stories can unite us across the tribal and physical barriers that would otherwise divide us.

Some of these stories are about God or the gods. Religion has played a crucial role in our species' development. It has united us, policed our behaviour, oriented our goals and provided comfort and hope in the face of life's unceasing trials and tragedies. But the "God story" is not the only story that has united us. Another much more recent tale is the story of human rights. Here's how Harari puts it:

> *"Most legal systems in the world today are based on a belief in human rights. But what are human rights? Human rights ... like God and heaven, are just a story that we've invented. They are not an objective reality. They're not a biological fact about Homo sapiens. Take a human being, cut him open, look inside; you will find the heart, the kidneys, neurons, hormones, DNA. But you won't find any rights. The only place you find rights*

is in the stories that we have invented and spread ...
over the last few centuries. They may be very positive
stories, very good stories. But they are still just fictional
stories that we've invented."[17]

What do you make of this argument? I think it gets
a number of things right. First, it draws attention to
the power of narrative. Undeniably our lives are given
meaning and perspective by the stories we tell ourselves.
Such stories build community, give a shared sense of value
and orient us to a common horizon. Second, Harari is
right to point to the similarities between the "God story"
and the "human rights story". As we'll see shortly, God
and human rights are inseparably linked (a point Harari
agrees with). Third, Harari is correct to say that rights are
not obvious or demonstrable scientifically. Our human
worth cannot be discovered via scientific experiments.
We share 40% of our DNA with bananas. This fact reveals
very little about the value of humans, or of bananas. DNA
does not and cannot confer moral worth. Someone with
Down's syndrome has an extra chromosome, but they are
no more or no less valuable for that.

Science tells us nothing about our equal status in relation
to one another. In fact, the more testing you do on a
population, the more you find differences between
people. Some are taller, some less so; some are smarter,
some less so; some are stronger, some less so. What we
see are differences. What we *seek* is equality. But we won't

17   Yuval Noah Harari, *What Explains the Rise of Humans*, Ted Talks, London 2015.
     https://www.ted.com/talks/yuval_noah_harari_what_explains_the_rise_of_
     humans/transcript. Accessed 27th October 2021.

find it—not anything morally significant—by mapping genomes, or running tests, or charting bell curves.

Harari is correct: human rights are found in the *stories* we tell. So what kind of story will suffice to establish our sense of human worth?

ELTON'S GLASS OF WATER

In 2018 Sam Harris and Jordan Peterson held a series of public debates which thousands attended and millions viewed online. Harris is a neuroscientist and best-selling author who has been dubbed one of the "four horsemen of the atheist apocalypse" (together with Richard Dawkins, Daniel Dennett and the late Christopher Hitchens). Peterson is a psychology professor, writer and popular YouTuber to whom we will return in chapter 10. In the second debate they discussed values and how we establish them. Harris put forward a memorable analogy. He picked up the glass of water next to him and said:

> *"What if I tell you this isn't just any glass. This is the glass Elton John drank from [when he was at this arena] at his last concert. How much do you want to pay me for it?"*[18]

This is a good example of how we value things. The glass by itself is worth very little—maybe a dollar. The glass *in connection with cultural icon Elton John* might be worth a thousand times as much. If the buyer values Elton John, then the buyer will also value the glass. But, asks Peterson,

---

18   "Sam Harris & Jordan Peterson in Vancouver - Part 2". Discussion held 24th June 2018. https://www.youtube.com/watch?v=GEf6X-FueMo. Accessed 29th October 2021.

"where is the value located?" The material contents of the glass are virtually worthless. But there's a story to be told about the glass. And in connection with that story—and with its hero, Elton John—the glass has a meaning far beyond its component parts.

During the debate, Harris takes the glass illustration in an interesting direction. He goes on to say that the glass is like a piece of land. In particular, he likens the glass to the strip of land at the eastern end of the Mediterranean— the land fought over by Jews and Palestinians alike. One group calls it "Israel" and another calls it "Palestine", but their conflict is motivated by stories—religious stories— told about the land. Harris despairs because he sees those stories as A) false and B) dangerous. They're dangerous because they cause people to assign to that piece of real estate a value far in excess of its worth.

> *"The reason why the parties involved in the Arab-Israeli conflict can't resolve their problems as though it were a real-estate transaction is because they are making irrational and irreconcilable claims [about the land]."*

So in Harris's telling, the glass is Israel/Palestine, and Elton John is "God"—a character in a story whose attachment to "the holy land" is inflating its value. The "God story" is to blame for the troubles. To finish off the analogy, Harris says:

> *"But while we're arguing over the value of the glass, Elton John was never here."*

The audience applaud loudly. In fact, modern people almost *have* to applaud this point. We shouldn't prize land over lives. It's not worth sacrificing people for Palestine/Israel. These are the kinds of slogans we can all get behind. But why can we get behind them? Because of another story we've told ourselves—a story about human value. That's the thing we value more than everything else: more than land, more than ideologies, more than made-up stories. We value people.

But this raises some bigger questions: *Why* do we value people? And how? Let's revisit the glass analogy and see what happens if the glass refers not to a piece of land but to the human person. Here's where an audience applauding Harris might find reason to think again.

Consider a human person. Consider their material contents. "What do you want to pay me for it?" Boil me down to my chemical makeup and I'm worth about 30 bucks. Or put me to work and maybe I'll earn you more. But is that my worth? And what about *your* value? Are you more or less worthwhile than me? Some bottles contain Perrier and some contain ditch water. Some glasses are crystal; some are paper cups. But is that how we want to value *people*?

The answer for most is no. We want to recognise a value in people that goes well beyond their material makeup or their economic utility. So what is it that stands outside the human person—something greater than humans but connected to them—which elevates their worth? Paging a cosmic Elton John: humanity needs you!

Perhaps it's becoming clear why the God story and the human-rights story are connected. Without a God story (and without a very particular God story), humans remain adrift in the world, fending for themselves and valued for their properties only—some valued more and some much less. But if there is an "Elton John figure", someone of supreme value, and if this source of value shares a vital connection to humanity, then another possibility is opened up. By association with God, we can see humans as worth far more than the flesh-and-blood material of each of us, and far more than our blood-and-sweat toil.

Of course the *kind* of God story we consult is all-important. None of the creation myths alluded to in the last chapter would be of much help in elevating the dignity of humanity. In those stories we are the products of violence and intended for slavery. But there exists a different story, with a different God and a very different outcome for the valuation of humans. The Bible's creation narrative may not strike us today as remarkable or revolutionary. But that can only be because we're unfamiliar with its ancient competitors or over-familiar with its modern consequences. Many of its assumptions have become the air we breathe. So let's give the ancient text a fresh look.

IN THE BEGINNING

"In the beginning, *Elohim*..." (Genesis 1:1). So starts the Bible. The grammar in the ancient Hebrew (the language in which the Old Testament was written) is unusual. *Elohim*, the Hebrew word for "God", is a plural noun, but it always goes with a singular verb. It would be a little like saying in English, "The dogs is barking". There's a strange interplay of plural and singular. And when it comes to God, the Bible continually brings this to our attention; there's something multiple about this God and something singular.

The biblical story is not about disparate deities—numerous gods at war with one another. Nor is it about a single tyrant—a divine dictator who stands alone, imposing his or her will. Nor is it about an impersonal force—a "thing" or an "it". Instead, the Bible is about a personal God who is a three-unity—in other words, a "tri-unity", or "Trinity". The Father, Son and Holy Spirit are one in the most profound sense. This is a unity across distinctions—a God who is love, as the Bible will later put it. Here is a unique conception of God and from this God comes a unique conception of creation.

According to the Hebrew Bible, it is this God, and this God alone, who "created the heavens and the earth" (Genesis 1:1). Here is another example of unity across difference. Ancient Hebrew, like modern languages such as French and German, uses grammatical genders. In this instance, the word for "heavens" is masculine and the word for "earth" is feminine. Upon hearing such a set-up, an ancient myth-lover may have anticipated a tale of sexual congress (or conquest) among the gods. Instead, heaven and earth—sky and land—face one another and await a different kind of love story. It's not the gods who will personify creation's romance; it's humanity. But we're getting ahead of ourselves. Soon we'll consider the romance; first we must explore the set-up.

In verse 2, we read of the "void", "darkness", and "the deep":

"Now the earth was formless and empty, darkness was over the surface of the deep, and the Spirit of God was hovering over the waters."

If we read this from the perspective of ancient peoples, we might here expect a battle. Perhaps the waters will writhe in rebellion. Perhaps the dark forces will conspire against one another. Perhaps war will break out and the victor gods will hurl their enemies into the deep. Yet in the biblical story there may be a primordial void, "formless and empty", but what fills it are not ambitious deities but a brooding "Spirit of God", patiently waiting. Waiting for what?

"And God said, 'Let there be light,' and there was light."

This story stands apart from the crowd, as does its God. In another tale the blank void would be a battleground; here it is a stage awaiting its actors. Then, like a spotlight, God's word enters the breach—unopposed and unwavering—and darkness flees. Light is victorious. Life is spoken.

And so it goes on in the verses that follow: day after day emptiness is filled, potential is formed, chaos is ordered. The heavens, the earth and the waters are commanded and, in obedience to the word of God, they shine, they sprout and they teem. There are no wars, no jealousies, no rebellion. There is a process—from simple to complex. There is progress—from dark emptiness to radiant abundance. Step by careful step, something is unfolding under the guidance of one creative Voice. In time the land and seas themselves bring forth life. Creation creates. Life gives life.

In the Bible the cosmos is not a machine, grinding along according to grim necessity. Nor is it a war zone, boiling with intrigue and violence. Nor is there a "click of the fingers" from a Magician on high. This is artistry, intended and loved. And at every turn the verdict is pronounced: "And God saw that it was good."

At the end of the process, we hear the emphatic declaration: "It was very good" (v 31). Why? Because the culmination of creation has arrived: humanity. The stage was being set all along. A space was being cleared: under heaven, upon the earth, and between the waters. Here comes the pinnacle of it all:

> "Then God said, 'Let us make mankind in our image, in our likeness, so that they may rule over the fish in the sea and the birds in the sky, over the livestock and all the wild animals, and over all the creatures that move along the ground.'
>
> "So God created mankind in his own image,
> in the image of God he created them;
> male and female he created them." (v 26-27)

On the first page of the Bible we might expect to hear how it is God who rules over the world. Yet this is humanity's role. Mankind is made not to slave but to reign. Male and female together are kings and queens of the cosmos and are stamped with the image and likeness of God.

Moderns may yawn at the idea, but ancients would choke on it. Male and female equally in God's image? Equally reigning over God's world? Unheard of! In other creation stories the *king* might be said to be an image of a god.

After all, tyrants portray well the kind of rule exercised by the gods. But in Genesis we have a very different picture of God and therefore of humanity. As another Hebrew Scripture would put it, "The highest heavens belong to the LORD, but the earth he has given to the human race" (Psalm 115:16). We have here the sense of blessing flowing from above: from heaven to earth *through* mankind. Dominion, not subjection, is our lot. And our *kind* of dominion is meant to be a picture of God's. In other words, it is meant to be power wielded for the benefit of those without it.

ASCENDING APES AND FALLEN ANGELS

Novelist Terry Pratchett summarised well two competing visions for humanity. Some consider us "ascending apes"; for others we are "fallen angels". Which is it?

Before picking a side, it's worth knowing that the Bible speaks to both visions. We are certainly frail, earth-bound, physical creatures, coming at the end of the creative process. In the poetic vision of Genesis 2, mankind is formed from the dust. Materially speaking we are base and brittle, and our lives are brief. But we are also breathed upon by God. There is bottom up ness to us and top-down-ness to us. We are dirt-bags kissed by heaven. Beloved dust. In ourselves we are like that one-dollar water glass. But we are touched by the divine too, and in connection with God we are precious beyond all earthly valuation. Precious, but profoundly flawed. That's the meaning of the next chapter of the story.

Genesis 3 describes what is often called "the fall". It's a fall from the light and life of the Bible's opening chapters into darkness and death. Everything had been harmonious, responding in obedience to the voice of God. Then Adam and Eve, the first humans, rebel against that voice—the command of God—and chaos ensues.

Notice how different this is from the other ancient stories. In those tales, mishaps and mayhem precede creation and pervade it necessarily. We could sing, along with Billy Joel, "we didn't start the fire". But Genesis sings a different song: humanity really did start the fire. We are not victims of the world; the world is a victim of us. Humanity was put at the helm of the good ship Earth, and it is we who ran it aground.

I admit this is a lot to swallow. My point here is not to convince you of the Genesis story but merely to show you the unparalleled role which humanity plays within it. Even when things fall apart, the Bible pays us the immense compliment of blaming us. Heaven and earth were made for a properly functioning humanity. Faulty humanity means a faulty world. In response to Adam and Eve's fall, the Lord details the consequences: toil at work, troubles at home, the battle of the sexes, the frustration of the earth, and our own mortality (Genesis 3:14-24). These are all laid at our door. Whatever you think of the plausibility or the proportionality of this, the scale of the disaster is a testament to the significance of the cause— the significance of *us*. There is profound importance attached to human dignity in the Bible, not merely as regards our dominion but also as regards our culpability. As rulers, as divine image-bearers, *and* as cosmic fire starters, humanity has the kind of significance reserved, in other religions, for the gods.

THE RADICAL ERROR

Late in the 2nd century, Celsus, one of Christianity's fiercest critics, said, "The radical error in Jewish and Christian thinking is that it is anthropocentric [human centred]. They say that God made all things for man, but this is not at all evident."[19] What was evident to Celsus was that "in no way is man better in God's sight than ants and bees". In this, Celsus was following in the footsteps of Plato. The notion that humans were different in kind from nature and from animals (a view sometimes called "human exceptionalism") was an affront to reason and nature. Therefore, Christians and Jews shared a root problem. Their radical error was that they were much, much too humanistic.

Of course, Christians only compounded the problem by insisting that the divine Son of God—described in the New Testament as "the Word" who made the world—became man (John 1:1-14). Celsus notes with horror that the Christian God "forsakes the whole universe and the course of the heavenly spheres to dwell with us alone".[20] If it was pride to think God specially blesses man, what kind of lunacy imagines that he *becomes* man? For Celsus this was nonsense. For a Christian, though, this is precisely what *makes* sense—of everything. If you believe that "man" (in the universal sense of the word) has been established to have "dominion", then of course the true King would show up as man. Of course he enters history, centre stage, in

---

19   Quoted in T.R. Glover, *The Conflict of Religions in the Early Roman Empire.* https://www.gutenberg.org/files/39092/39092-h/39092-h.htm (para. 244). Accessed 29th October 2021.

20   Quoted in Larry Siedentop, *Inventing the Individual* (Penguin, 2015), p 71.

this way. Humanity is the location he prepared for himself right back "in the beginning". To become human is exactly the sort of thing *this* God would do. And he did it so as to take the wheel of his own world and guide creation home.

The view which Celsus called an error would go on to win the day. The inherent value of each human, made "in the image of God", is right at the root of our modern view of the world. From the time of Celsus onwards, history has witnessed the overturning of his assumptions and the establishment of Christian ones. Now human equality, human rights and human*ism* can trace their sources back to this biblical root.

This of course raises the question: without such a belief, what might remain of human rights and equality?

If you consult Celsus, he will answer from the perspective of the classical world: *Quit your human-centredness! The gods are indifferent, and nature is unequal.*

If you consult Harari, he will answer from our modern understanding: *The struggle for survival is indifferent and viciously unequal. Human rights are as fictional as the God who underwrites them.*

Both men though, ancient and modern, are correct in this: the God story and the equality story stand or fall together. If we feel that life is sacred, that every human possesses an inviolable dignity and equality, and that no one deserves to be trampled down simply because they are smaller or weaker or poorer, then we are standing on particularly biblical foundations. There is a thread running from Genesis through the New Testament to our 21st-century humanist convictions. In the coming chapters we will trace out the developments in more detail, but for now it's enough to know that the thread is strong. It needs to be—the modern world hangs by it.

3. COMPASSION

"Abort it and try again. It would be immoral to bring it into the world if you have the choice."

— Richard Dawkins, 2014

The advice came in 2014 from the eminent biologist and the world's most famous atheist, Richard Dawkins. The occasion was a question on Twitter from a woman who said that discovering Down's syndrome in any future pregnancy would present her with "a real ethical dilemma": whether to abort or not.

Dawkins' clear-eyed exhortation, offered without hesitation, cut through the questioner's qualms and attracted an onslaught of online outrage. Comparisons with eugenics and Nazi ideology were swift in coming, and, as is often the case in these incidents, the subsequent apology only made things worse. Dawkins clarified that he was only advising a course of action which the great majority of parents in this position do in fact take. He could have added that his advice would have found hearty approval from the ancient world.

Plato thought that in order to be worth rearing, children must be "malleable, disposed to virtue and physically fit".[21] If they did not prove themselves worthy, parents

---

21 A summary of Plato's teaching from Darrel W. Amundsen in "Medicine and

would "properly dispose of [them] in secret, so that no one will know what has become of them."[22] Aristotle thought defective children should be exposed—that is, discarded at rubbish tips, abandoned on hillsides, thrown down wells or drowned in rivers. "As to exposing or rearing the children born, let there be a law that no deformed child shall be reared."[23] In other words, it would be immoral not to do this. Infanticide was so widespread in the Roman world (in fact, in all the world) that the first known treatise on gynaecology included the vital section "How to Recognise the Newborn That is Worth Rearing".[24] If they did not make the grade, the advice was "Expose it and try again".

Around the world and down through history the vast majority of cultures have considered that we are all better off without the weak. In our own society, advanced technology means that recognition and disposal of so-called "inferior offspring" can happen ever earlier, *in utero* even. But the furore over Richard Dawkins' position points to a deep instinct within us. Even when, nowadays, we seek and destroy the disabled as secretly and clinically as possible, we nevertheless cannot escape feeling that

the Birth of Defective Children: Approaches of the Ancient World" in *On Moral Medicine: Theological Perspectives in Medical Ethics*, edited Stephen E. Lammers and Allen Verhey (Eerdmans, 1998), p 682.

22 Plato, *Republic*, Book 5, p 460. http://www.perseus.tufts.edu/hopper/text?doc=Pe rseus%3Atext%3A1999.01.0168%3Abook%3D5%3Apage%3D460. Accessed 29th October 2021.

23 Aristotle, *Politics*, Book 7, section 1335b.

24 Soranus of Ephesus (98-138) wrote a chapter "On the Care of the Newborn", which begins with the section "How To Recognise the Newborn That is Worth Rearing", in *Gynecology* (trans. Owsei Temkin, Johns Hopkins University Press, 1991), p 79.

our moral imperative is to protect the weak, not eliminate them. Where does this come from?

THE POISON OF PITY

Friedrich Nietzsche (1844–1900) identified the culprit in his book *The Anti-Christ*. The problem, according to the German philosopher, was the poison of pity. "Pity on the whole thwarts the law of evolution, which is the law of selection."[25] In other words, nature selects the strong and eliminates the weak. Who are we to disobey this law—a law that has given us life?

Notice how, for Nietzsche, the word "law" does double duty. It is both a description of biological reality and a prescription for ethical living. If the fittest do survive (a scientific law), then the fittest *should* survive (a moral law). Nietzsche called this resolve to follow the law of evolution, "the first principle of our philanthropy". Philanthropy is the love of humanity. Nietzsche believed he was loving humanity best by identifying and enforcing the realities of natural selection. "The weak and ill-constituted shall perish" Nietzsche decreed before adding, "and one shall help them to do so".[26]

If we recoil from such ruthless behaviour, (and Nietzsche knew we would), it's only because we are captive to "life's nausea": in other words, Christianity.

> *"Christianity has taken the part of all the weak, the low, the botched; it has made an ideal out of antagonism to*

25 Friedrich Nietzsche, *The Anti-Christ*, Aphorism 7. Found in *Writings of Nietzsche*, Col. 1, edited Anthony Uyl (Devoted Publishing, 2016), p 122.

26 As above, p 121.

all the self-preservative instincts of sound life."[27]

To translate, Christians have put themselves on the side of the inferior, endangering the survival of the species. What is worse, from Nietzsche's point of view, is that they have disguised this betrayal of humanity as a virtue. As he says elsewhere, Christianity is "disgust with life ... dressed up as faith".[28] Christians oppose the self-preservation of humanity, they oppose its evolution towards greatness, and then they have the audacity to call this an "ideal". Surely the "sound" course of action is to protect ourselves from "the botched"? Yet Christians intervene with their anti-life, unnatural ethic of compassion.

Nietzsche was correct to identify Christianity as the champion of pity in our midst. It is Christianity that informs our instincts regarding the protection and nurture of the weak. Without the Jesus movement, it is difficult to imagine Richard Dawkins' tweet prompting much more than "Thx. Will do. xx"

But if we want to listen more closely to our moral sensibilities here, if we want to avoid Nietzsche's conclusions regarding the weak and "botched", if we consider pity a virtue and not a weakness, and if we reckon that the best societies protect their weakest members (rather than eliminate them), we will need to erect the strongest firewall between scientific law and moral law. That is, we will need to keep science as science and morality as morality.

---

27   As above, p 122.

28   Friedrich Nietzsche, *The Birth of Tragedy* (Random House, 1967), p 23.

Deriving the latter from the former is fraught with trouble. Science observes the ruthless winnowing of the weak and the favouring of the strong. If this is the way of nature, what reason can we give for behaving any differently? "There is nothing particular about man. He is but a part of this world," said Heinrich Himmler, the chief architect of the Holocaust.[29] If we are simply a part of nature—and if there is nothing above nature—then what can we do but live according to nature? And we know what nature does: it selects the strong and discards the weak.

To avoid such genocidal conclusions, we need a morality that is beyond nature, above nature—something supernatural, you might say. And in history there has been a unique movement that transcends the brutal laws of nature. If natural selection means the survival of the fittest and the sacrifice of the weakest, Christianity is about the sacrifice of the Fittest (Jesus Christ) for the survival of the weakest (us). It is a moral revolution, confounding the Nietzsches of the world and giving hope to the "botched". The centre of this revolution is a unique vision of God.

TO IMAGE GOD

"What does it look like when God shows up?" This was the title of a sermon I preached as a guest speaker at an unfamiliar church. They clearly possessed a zealous publicist because when I arrived, there stood outside

---

29 Heinrich Himmler, quoted by Tom Holland in *Dominion* (Little, Brown, 2019), p 521.

the building a large sign with the words "What Does It Look Like When God Shows Up?" So far so good. Unfortunately, next to the question there appeared—as if by way of an answer—a picture of my face. This could only be a profound disappointment to people. Or a blasphemy. Does God look like a middle-aged Australian with a crooked nose? If not, then what does God look like? Or, to put it another way, what could possibly be an *image* or *likeness* of God?

If you had asked someone from the ancient Near East, they might have answered, "The king". After all, the deities were themselves despotic tyrants. If you had asked a Greek philosopher, "What images God?" they might have replied, "The universe". Plato imagined that the world we see is a shadowy image cast by an original divine light.

But with the Bible in hand, the answer to the question "What images God?" is extraordinary: us. As we saw in the last chapter, human beings, both male and female, bear the image and likeness of God. It's not really that God is like us, it's that we are like God. Here, on page one of the Bible, lies a treasure more valuable than all the world because we are said to be more valuable than all the world. This is a status given not according to a person's strength, rank, race or gender but simply on account of belonging to the human family.

According to the Bible, Heinrich Himmler was wrong. We are more than "a part of this world"; we have dominion over the world. Humanity was made to stand between heaven and earth—commissioned from above to care for that which is below. The kindness of God therefore flows down and out.

"Down and out" describes the direction of travel for God's love, but it's also a good description of its typical recipient. Later in the Bible story, when God comes to select his "chosen people"—the ancient Israelites—he makes sure to underline his reasons:

> "The LORD your God has chosen you out of all the peoples on the face of the earth to be his people, his treasured possession. The LORD did not set his affection on you and choose you because you were more numerous than other peoples, for you were the fewest of all peoples. But it was because the LORD loved you ... and redeemed you from the land of slavery, from the power of Pharaoh king of Egypt." (Deuteronomy 7:6-8)

God loved helpless Israel, and his love met them precisely when they were "down and out" in Egypt. Israel's redemption from slavery, known as the exodus, was the definitive act of the Old Testament. In delivering the people from their captors and bringing them through the Red Sea, God was saving a despised and helpless people from the superpower of their day, and delivering them into the promised land—a land "flowing with milk and honey".

He did not do this because they were more impressive or worthy than others. He loved the loveless to make them lovely and to make them bearers of his love to the world. Compassion drove it all. This is the pattern for all of God's activity in the Bible: compassion that flows "down and out". And it flows *to* the "down and outs". It meets the people in their weakness and then raises them up so they might share the blessings far and wide.

As the Hebrew Bible (also known as the "Old Testament") continues, we see the way in which God works decisively through the "down and outs". While other nations would boast in their kings, precious few of Israel's heroes were kings, and precious few of their kings were heroes. Even their very best rulers (David and Solomon) were known as much for their failures as for their feats. Other armies would boast in their battles; Israel was a minnow whose greatest victories were won with slingshots, trumpets and tent pegs (1 Samuel 17; Judges 7; Judges 4). Other kingdoms would sing of their greatness; Israel's songs were full of their faults. To seek glory and greatness was, for many in the ancient world, the very meaning of their existence. In contrast the Jews were told by their God, "Do you seek great things for yourself? Seek them not" (Jeremiah 45:5, ESV). Among the jostling empires of the world, Israel was, on every level, an enigma.

From the 8th century BC to the 1st, the Israelites were swallowed up and spat out by superpower after superpower—the Assyrians, the Babylonians, the Medes and Persians, the Greeks and then the Romans—yet they never lost the sense that they were God's chosen agents of redemption and hope. As "people of the book", they possessed something—the instructions and the promises of God—which could never be destroyed. And in the fullness of time, the promise of all promises would appear: the Messiah.

Isaiah (c. 8th century BC), along with many other

prophets, spoke of this coming king—the "anointed one" who had been chosen to reign (the Hebrew word is "Messiah"; the Greek word is "Christ"). In chapter 61 we read one of many prophecies where Isaiah anticipates the Messiah's words:

> "The Spirit of the Sovereign LORD is on me,
>   because the LORD has anointed me
> to proclaim good news to the poor.
>   He has sent me to bind up the broken-hearted,
> to proclaim freedom for the captives,
>   and release from darkness for the prisoners,
> to proclaim the year of the LORD's favour."
>
> (Isaiah 61:1-2)

Here was the deepest hope of God's people: the coming of the Messiah—compassion incarnate.

COMPASSION INCARNATE

When he arrived, the Messiah both fulfilled and defied expectations. The long-awaited King looked nothing like the kings we are used to. For one thing, Jesus was a nobody from a nowhere town. To place him in an equivalent modern setting, Rowan Williams, the former Archbishop of Canterbury, asks us to imagine a car mechanic from Basra during the US occupation of Iraq.[30] Let's develop the analogy: Jesus is like a car mechanic who preaches peace to all sides of the conflict and ends up tortured to death in Abu Ghraib, the notorious detention centre. In fact, let's develop the analogy even further: Jesus is like an Iraqi

---

30   Rowan Williams, *Tokens of Trust: An Introduction to Christian Belief* (Canterbury Press, 2007), p 68.

torture victim left to rot in a forgotten hell hole, who, soon after his shameful death, is worshipped as the Lord and Saviour of the world. He's *that* kind of torture victim.

Everything the New Testament tells us about Jesus' life screams paradox. He was the divine Word of God, who spoke with a much-scorned northern accent (John 1:1; Matthew 26:73). He was the cosmic King, who took the form of a slave (Philippians 2:7). He was the Maker of the world, whose day job was making furniture—until one day, aged 30, he put away the hammer, took up a scroll and preached to a small-town congregation. His inaugural address was a sermon from Isaiah 61 (the quotation above). Upon finishing the reading he told them all, "Today this scripture is fulfilled in your hearing" (Luke 4:21).

The claim was stratospherically lofty: he considered himself the fulfilment of prophecy, the bringer of good news, the healer of broken hearts, the liberator of the oppressed—in short, the Messiah. The audience, for their part, tried to kill him, and Jesus had to escape an early martyrdom. This was how it went for Jesus for the next three years until his enemies finally (and literally) pinned him down. He brought a message of hope and reconciliation while his hearers brought hostility and rejection. It's a clash which Jesus met, characteristically, with "compassion".

In the Gospels (the biographies of Christ's life), the word that describes Jesus' emotional life more than any other is "compassion". The authors had to reach for an odd Greek word to describe his depth of feeling: a verb form of the word for "intestines". When describing love, we moderns speak romantically of "the heart", but ancient people knew that the deepest feelings are experienced in our innards. And such stomach-churning pity was so obvious in Jesus that the Gospel writers continually spoke of it. When he brought healing (Matthew 20:34), restoration (Mark 1:41), or new life (Luke 7:13), we are told that he was moved with [gut-level] compassion. When he placed himself as a character in his parables (his spiritual stories), he made sure to reveal his inward motivations. Like a merciful ruler forgiving an enormous debt, like a merciful father restoring a wretched son, like a good Samaritan rescuing a dying man, Jesus is full of gut-wrenching love: "compassion" (Matthew 18:27; Luke 15:20; 10:33).

That last parable, the Good Samaritan, is perhaps Christ's best known (Luke 10:25-37). It tells of a man left for dead by robbers. Two religious leaders walk by on the other side of the road. Only a despised Samaritan (a man from another nation and religion) is moved with compassion. He stops, stoops, cares for the man and carries him to a make-shift hospital, paying for the full treatment of this stranger. It's a picture of Christ's own stooping love. It's also a challenge to all who would follow him: "Go and do likewise" (v 37).

Compassion describes the life of Christ, and it's meant to describe the life of the Christian. But these were incredibly strange ideas to Roman ears. We might be familiar with the idea that God loves the world (whether or not we believe in God or his love), but the historian Larry Hurtado calls the notion, "utterly strange, even ridiculous ... in the Roman era."[31] We take for granted the idea of a "love ethic", but historians "simply do not know of any other Roman-era religious group in which love played this important role in discourse or behavioral teaching".

Roman religion was different. They already had a "son of God": the emperor. Caesar Augustus (27 BC – AD 14) was called "Lord", "Saviour of the world" and "Son of God". The "God" whose son he was (by adoption) was Julius Caesar, whose claims to divinity included killing a million Gauls and enslaving a million more. (For Gaul, think France.) That was Caesar's boast, anyway. But, whatever the true figure, we should note that it was considered a boast and not a blemish. Here was evidence of his greatness— indeed of his godness.

Christ's brush with imperial power was the polar opposite. At the crucifixion, as a spear was thrust into Christ's side to finish the job, we see two very different pictures of greatness. At one end of the spear was a centurion, enforcing imperial might. At the other end was Jesus, a despised but innocent victim of injustice.

So at which end of the spear is true greatness to be found? Glory? Power? The apostle Paul spoke for all Christians when he declared that *Jesus* was "the image of the invisible God ... making peace through his blood, shed on the cross" (Colossians 1:15, 20). According to the Bible, you've never seen anything more divine than that crucified man. Here is love at full strength: the highest ruler plunging to the deepest depths in order to

---

31 Larry Hurtado, *Destroyer of the Gods* (Baylor University Press, 2017), p 64-65.

embrace the world. In peacemaking sacrifice, with arms outstretched even to his enemies, this is what it looks like to be God.

COMPASSION SHARED

With such a picture of "compassion incarnate" at its heart, it's no surprise that the Jesus movement sought to learn from the good Samaritan and "go and do likewise". Care for the sick became a characteristically *Christian* thing.

Medical care did not, of course, originate with Christians. The Greeks had their physicians and manuals. The Romans had their "sick bays" for slaves and soldiers. But such sick bays existed in order to return the injured to economic and military usefulness. Christians, following the lead of the good Samaritan, developed something new: healthcare for all. The religious scholar David Bentley Hart gives a sketch of the early development:

"St. Ephraim the Syrian (A.D. c. 306-373), when the city of Edessa was ravaged by plague, established hospitals open to all who were afflicted. St. Basil the Great (A.D. 329-379) founded a hospital in Cappadocia with a ward set aside for the care of lepers, whom he did not disdain to nurse with his own hands. St. Benedict of Nursia (A.D. c. 480 – c. 547) opened a free infirmary at Monte Cassino and made care of the sick a paramount duty of his monks. In Rome, the Christian noblewoman and scholar St. Fabiola (d. A.D. c. 399) established the first public hospital in Western Europe and—despite her wealth and position—often ventured out into the streets personally to seek out those who needed care. St. John Chrysostom (A.D. 347-407), while patriarch of

Constantinople, used his influence to fund several such institutions in the city."[32]

This care for the poor and sick was headed up by church leaders. Charity was considered integral to the faith and to the duties of each Christian, with the bishops leading the way. They presided over "mini welfare states", with their size and infrastructure further growing after the conversion of the Roman emperor Constantine in 312.[33]

From the 5th century there was, to use medievalist James William Brodman's phrase, a "cascade of hospitals".[34] In the Middle Ages, just the monastic order of the Benedictines alone were responsible for more than 2,000 hospitals in western Europe.[35] These movements were thoroughly and particularly Christian. Today, if you need first aid, look for a white cross on a green background— the internationally recognised sign. If you're in a crisis, it's the "Red Cross" which millions turn to—a charity whose strapline sounds suspiciously like a summary of Jesus' famous parable: "Refusing to ignore people in crisis". The good Samaritan lives. In fact nowadays the good Samaritan is assumed.

But there's nothing natural about this. Nature is "red in tooth and claw", as the poet Tennyson put it.[36] Compassion comes from another realm. It is, in a real sense, "super-natural".

---

32   David Bentley Hart, *Atheist Delusions* (Yale University Press, 2010), p 30.

33   Larry Siedentop, *Inventing the Individual* (Penguin, 2015), p 81.

34   Quoted in John Dickson, *Bullies and Saints* (Zondervan, 2021), p 191.

35   David Bentley Hart, *Atheist Delusions* (Yale University Press, 2010), p 30.

36   "In Memoriam A.H.H" (1850).

SUPER-NATURAL

I realise that word might put some people off. *Who, these days, believes in the "supernatural"?* Where's the evidence? But belief in the supernatural is everywhere. It is evident in every objection to Richard Dawkins' tweet. It is at work whenever we recoil from Nietzsche's pitiless philosophy. It appears whenever Jesus Christ is considered a superior model of greatness to Julius Caesar. If you reckon there are values like compassion that are above and beyond "the law of selection" and that those should take precedence in the event of a clash, then you believe in the supernatural. And at that point the Christian comes along and says, *Where is your evidence?*

For what it's worth, here is some of the evidence a Christian might cite for *their* view: in the 1st century some remarkable values were injected into a brutal world— values that continue to shape us today. These values had been prefigured in the Hebrew Bible, but something happened to make compassion burst the banks of Israel and begin to flood the world.

Christians have an explanation for this. We say that kindness appeared in the world because Kindness *himself* appeared—kindness enfleshed (Titus 3:4). Jesus is Pity with a capital P. He entered the pitiless realm of nature and suffered its brutalities. Yet in love, he chose the cross. And it was on the cross that Christ, the Fittest, was sacrificed for us, the weakest, so that we, the weakest, might survive—more than that, that we might be raised up, forgiven and filled with the life of his Spirit.

This is the message that birthed the Jesus movement of the 1st century. Naturally, human movements will be based on human achievements and distinctives. But this is a movement of the Spirit, and it operates on a "down and out" basis, using whatever strengths it receives to serve those without them.

What does such a movement look like? Jesus spelt out the distinctiveness to his earliest followers:

> "You know that those who are regarded as rulers of the Gentiles [the non-Jewish nations] lord it over them, and their high officials exercise authority over them. Not so with you. Instead whoever wants to become great among you must be your servant, and whoever wants to be first must be slave of all. For even the Son of Man [that is, Jesus himself] did not come to be served, but to serve, and to give his life as a ransom for many." (Mark 10:42-45)

Today we take it for granted that "lording it over others" is a bad look. Among management consultants, "servant leadership" is so commonplace as to be clichéd. Facebook memes abound declaring, "A society should be judged by the treatment of its weakest members". And in many a Christianised country we call our leaders "ministers"—literally it's the old English for "servant". In the UK, our chief governor is called the *prime* minister—first in the queue to minister to us. If you want evidence of the Christian revolution, look no further: our rulers used to pronounce themselves "Gods"; now they are servants.

Of course, the leaders themselves have a very mixed record as regards their Christ-like compassion. Their people likewise struggle. But the values by which we judge them remain. Kindness has caught on.

GLADIATORS, GARBAGE DUMPS AND GOD

"You do not attend our shows, you take no part in the processions, you are not present at our public banquets, you abhor the sacred [i.e. gladiatorial] games."[37]

This complaint, addressed to the first Christians, was typical of the way Roman citizens felt about the burgeoning Jesus movement. Christians were a maddening mystery. They boycotted blood sports, they shunned displays of civic worship, and they refused to worship the emperor (since Christ alone is Lord). For this the Romans considered them enemies of humanity, and so while Christians would refuse to *attend* the gladiatorial games, sometimes they would become the entertainment: fed to the beasts. As they died, though, with dignity and determination, the thousands who came to see one kind of glory got a glimpse of another. In the arena, the violence of empire was met by sacrificial love. Christ's way of the Spirit flowed on.

It took until AD 401 for the games to be finally outlawed by an edict of the Christian emperor Honorius. (As we will see, spiritual realities take time to be grasped by individuals and churches, and they can take centuries to take root in rulers and empires.) Nevertheless, as historian William Lecky has argued, "There is scarcely any reform

---

37 Marcus Minucius Felix, *Octavius 12*, quoted in Alvin J. Schmidt, *Under the Influence: How Christianity Transformed Civilization* (Zondervan, 2001), p 25.

so important in the moral history of mankind as the suppression of the Gladiatorial games, a feat that must be almost exclusively ascribed to the Christian Church."[38]

Fittingly, the story surrounding their abolition involved a martyr. Emperor Honorius was moved, so it was said, by the efforts of a monk named Telemachus, who entered the arena one day with the goal of stopping the slaughter. The monk stood between the gladiators but was stoned to death by the angry crowd. There is power, though, in sacrifice—power to overturn fear and violence. As his example sank in with the masses and as his story reached the ears of the emperor, so there came a revolution. As with the Lord whom he followed, Telemachus' bloodshed was turned to blessing, his sacrifice changed hearts, his death made peace, and his martyrdom proved victorious.

A similar story can be told about ending the exposure of infants. Once again the early Christians made known their implacable opposition to the practice, and at the same time they demonstrated sacrificial love in addressing it. Right from the beginning the early church took up collections for the poor and sick, not just their own but those of the surrounding culture. Such charitable giving beyond the family and beyond the clan was extremely rare in the ancient world. In time, the bishops of the early churches presided over their "welfare distribution centres", with hospitals and orphanages rising up to meet the needs.[39] It was this combination of word and deed

---

38 Quoted in Phillip Schaff, *History of the Christian Church*, §95. https://www.ccel.org/ccel/schaff/hcc2.v.x.viii.html. Accessed 30th October 2021.

39 John Dickson, *Bullies and Saints* (Zondervan, 2021), p 33-36, 74-76.

which later saw legislation catching up. In the late 4th century, the Christian emperor Valentinian I made it a law that parents rear their own children, and he forbade the killing of an infant. But culturally what made the enduring difference was not the changes in law but the changes in hearts. A new kind of heroism had gripped the world. It was evident in monks like Telemachus or nuns like Macrina (330–379), whose life of radical generosity included touring the rubbish dumps to rescue exposed infants and adopt them into her community.

These were the stories that captured the imagination because at the heart of the faith was the original Martyr, the stooping God. He is the kind of God who descends to the garbage dump (that was, after all, where the Romans would routinely set up their crucifixions). And this wasn't just an Easter reality. Jesus pointed his followers to the starving, the immigrant, the sick and the imprisoned, saying, *Whatever you do for the least of these, you do for me* (Matthew 25:40).

What was Macrina looking for in the garbage dump? The deepest answer is God. And in among "the weak, the low and the botched", she, and the many she's inspired, found him.

It turns out the supernatural really does show up, and when it does, it looks exactly like sacrificial love.

4. CONSENT

"How much is a little girl worth?"

— Rachael Denhollander, 2018

Rachael Denhollander was the last of 169 women to give her victim-impact statement. Years earlier she had been among the first to go public about serial sexual predator Larry Nassar.

Nassar had abused at least 265 girls over the course of decades as a medical professional. As the team doctor for USA Gymnastics he used his position to exploit women and girls in his care. But as the judge considered sentencing, Denhollander, a survivor of Nassar's abuse and an attorney in her own right, wanted the court's attention drawn to one question: "How much is a little girl worth?"

As she concluded her extraordinary 37-minute testimony, she addressed the judge:

> *"Judge Aquilina, I plead with you as you deliberate the sentence to give Larry, send a message that these victims are worth everything ... I plead with you to impose the maximum sentence under the plea agreement because everything is what these survivors are worth. Thank you."*[40]

---

40 "Read Rachael Denhollander's Full Victim Impact Statement about Larry Nassar", CNN, 30th January 2018. https://edition.cnn.com/2018/01/24/us/rachael-

Soon after Denhollander's statement, the judge imposed multiple prison sentences on Nassar of between 40 and 175 years, in addition to the 60-year sentence he had already received. "I just signed your death warrant," said the judge, acknowledging that Nassar would never again walk free. The message was sent: girls—victims, survivors, the vulnerable—are worth *everything*.

It should be said that the justice system rarely delivers this kind of verdict on behalf of survivors. In the UK, it is estimated that for every 200 reports of rape only three make it to trial.[41] But there is, at least, an expectation that Denhollander's question will provoke serious soul searching. How much is a little girl worth? We want to answer, *"Everything"*. The fact that 1 in 4 women and 1 in 6 men will experience sexual abuse before the age of 18 breaks our hearts. Paedophilia is regarded as the most dreadful crime and, among prisoners, sex offenders are considered the lowest of the low. While today these attitudes are considered to be some of the most basic, universal and obvious values imaginable, they are, historically, nothing of the sort.

If you asked a Roman, "How much is a little girl worth?", they might have offered a number of answers. She's free if you manage to salvage her as a baby from the rubbish heap where she was exposed. If slave-traders got to her first, then you'd have to pay them perhaps eight

---

denhollander-full-statement/index.html. Accessed 10th November 2021.

41 "Just 1.5% of all rape cases lead to charge or summons, data reveals", the Guardian, 26th July 2019. https://www.theguardian.com/law/2019/jul/26/rape-cases-charge-summons-prosecutions-victims-england-wales. Accessed 30th October 2021.

month's wages to own her.[42] Once yours, though, her body belongs to you outright: "It is accepted that every master is entitled to use his slave as he desires."[43] If, though, you wanted a girl purely on a pay-as-you-go basis, prostitution was, in the words of historian Kyle Harper, "a dominant institution, flourishing in the light of day. The sex industry was integral to the moral economy of the classical world."[44] A quick visit to the nearest brothel (and they were everywhere), would set you back the price of a loaf of bread.[45]

So how much is a little girl worth? We answer, "Everything". Others in history would laugh at us, all the way to the brothel. Why the difference? In a word: Christianity.

INVENTING ABUSE

A number of Christians have been found guilty of horrendous sexual crimes in the last 20 centuries. Some have gained the headlines, while others have not, and sometimes the cover-ups have been as diabolical as the abuse. But there is more than one sense in which Christianity has brought abuse into the world. The Christian revolution has given us the category for sexual abuse—a category that was unknown to the culture in which Christianity first spread. Kyle Harper writes of the Roman world, "The complete, violent exploitation of

42 *The Slave Systems of Greek and Roman Antiquity*, American Philosophical Society (William Linn Westermann, 1957), p 100.

43 Quoted in Tom Holland, *Dominion* (Little, Brown, 2019), p 99.

44 Kyle Harper, *Shame to Sin* (Harvard University Press, 2016), p 3.

45 As above, p 49.

women without any claim to civic protection was simply, as a problem in its own right, invisible."[46] In other words, our modern concept of sexual abuse would be nonsensical to a freeborn Roman man since he considered that he held an unquestioned right to the bodies of lower-status women, children, prostitutes and slaves. What we might call "abuse" was, to his mind, the obvious *use* for sex.

"In the sexual life of the Roman Empire, it would be impossible to overstate the decisive influence of social position in the determination of sexual boundaries."[47] It was the status of your partner—not their consent, their age or their gender—that mattered. And it was your reputation within a shame-based culture that determined the rightness of an encounter, not any inherent wrongfulness regarding particular acts. It was, to use Harper's phrase, a world of shame, not of sin. What mattered was "loss of face" rather than violation of a law, still less of a body. If your partner was already degraded socially—and who was not the inferior of a male Roman citizen?—they could not themselves suffer loss. They were fair game.

Certainly some people were off limits—highborn women and wives had to have their chastity protected at all costs. There was a flagrant and unapologetic double standard for men and women. Even the key word regarding sexual morality—"modesty"—meant something different depending on your gender. For a woman "modesty" meant faithfulness within marriage and virginity before

---

46   As above, p 8.

47   As above, p 8.

it (though they would not have to wait long—marriages at the age of 12 were common). A man was expected to honour the modesty of those women who possessed it. (Slaves and prostitutes naturally lacked this virtue.)

All this meant that adultery—sleeping with another man's wife—was a very serious crime, but it was not a crime of passion. Given the free availability of sex via the flesh trade, adultery was usually politically rather than erotically charged. It was a heinous slight against the husband and a transgression of the social order. The adulterer destroyed their own "sense of shame, orderly self-control, citizenship, neighborliness".[48] Men, therefore, were called to a certain moderation in their appetites. Indeed, that is what the word "modesty" meant for *male* sexual ethics—not chastity but self-control. What this meant in practice was that slaves and prostitutes were used frequently as a sop for the lusts of men so that they wouldn't indulge them with married women. A trip to the brothel might well be taken *in the name of* modesty—the male variety, anyway.

Some philosophers counselled more moderation than others. A reputation for self-control was important lest you invite the charge of "softness" or "effeminacy". Thus, the super-strict might exhort the super-virtuous to forswear all sex beyond procreation, as did the Stoic philosopher Musonius Rufus. But all of this still assumed the classical outlook on sex, gender, status and bodies. Such teaching was not a challenge to the natural order; it was simply a challenge to certain men to exercise

---

48 As above, p 56.

impressive levels of self-control. And very few rose to the challenge. There is a reason why Latin has 25 words for a prostitute and none for a *male* virgin.[49] Those two facts were very much linked.

Tom Holland has summarised the prevailing outlook:

> *"Sex was nothing if not an exercise of power. As captured cities were to the swords of the legions, so the bodies of those used sexually were to the Roman man. To be penetrated, male or female, was to be branded as inferior: to be marked as womanish, barbarian, servile ... In Rome, men no more hesitated to use slaves and prostitutes to relieve themselves of their sexual needs than they did to use the side of a road as a toilet. In Latin, the same word, meio, meant both ejaculate and urinate."*[50]

The very things that strike us as abusive—the power-plays, the inequality, the objectification, the clinical use of bodies and persons—were in fact presumed in the sexual morality of the day. It was business as usual. Then came the sexual revolution.

THE SEXUAL REVOLUTION

When we think of the "sexual revolution", our minds turn instantly to the 1960s. It was a time after contraception became available, and before AIDS emerged, when sex was made much less consequential, at least as regards pregnancy. The sexes were equalised. Women could

---

49   Joseph Henrich, *The Weirdest People in the World* (Penguin, 2020), p 167.

50   Tom Holland, *Dominion* (Little, Brown, 2019), p 99.

experience the same kinds of sexual licence as men had, and, in the aftermath, sex, marriage, the family, and much more underwent radical change.

Nineteen centuries before "the summer of love", another revolution in sexual values and practices was unleashed on the world—and its impact was even more transformative. That 1st-century sexual revolution has given the world certain understandings of sex, love, freedom, choice, the body, the family, gender and equality which remain operative today, even among those who consider themselves free from the church's strictures. But the relationship between these two revolutions is revealing. In many ways, "the swinging sixties" were the mirror image of that 1st-century revolution.

In the 1960s, there was a concern for gender equality, and so social taboos around female sexuality were relaxed. In the early church, there was a similar concern for gender equality, but the double standard was attacked from the other side. The church imposed restrictions on men— the same restrictions that had always limited women. If the revolution of the 20th century said, *Women can be as free as men*, the Jesus revolution had said, *Men must be as restricted as women*. Given the complete sexual dominance of men in the ancient world, the coup was as audacious as it was transformative.

LIVE LIKE EUNUCHS

If Christianity brought an earthquake in sexual morality, then Matthew 19 is the epicentre. The chapter begins with Israel's strictest religionists, the Pharisees, asking Jesus about divorce and remarriage. In the Roman world divorce was easy. Among Jews there was debate about how difficult it should be. Jesus outflanked everyone with the strictest regime ever imposed on men.

Some Pharisees came to him to test him. They asked, "Is it lawful for a man to divorce his wife for any and every reason?"

> "'Haven't you read,' he replied, 'that at the beginning the Creator "made them male and female," and said, "For this reason a man will leave his father and mother and be united to his wife, and the two will become one flesh"? So they are no longer two, but one flesh. Therefore what God has joined together, let no one separate.'" (Matthew 19:3-6)

When Jesus references "the beginning", he is taking his hearers back to the Bible's first chapters: Genesis 1 and 2. Here, the phrase "one flesh" describes two things: a union of bodies (sex) and a union of lives (marriage). In the Bible, sex is marital and marriage is sexual. The one-flesh act (sex) belongs in the one-flesh union (marriage).

There is, therefore, an intense significance to sex on the human level. Our sexual partner should be our life partner. But Jesus adds a vertical dimension too. When speaking of marriage, he speaks of "what God has joined together". Apparently, what we do with our flesh is also *spiritual*. Our human partnerships are not just human. They matter to God.

Such teaching represents the death of "casual sex". It's also the death of easy divorce, and so Jesus' questioners press him by appealing to their ancestor Moses and the laws he gave Israel in the Old Testament:

"'Why then,' they asked, 'did Moses command that a man give his wife a certificate of divorce and send her away?'

"Jesus replied, 'Moses permitted you to divorce your wives because your hearts were hard. But it was not this way from the beginning. I tell you that anyone who divorces his wife, except for sexual immorality, and marries another woman commits adultery.'"

(Matthew 19:7-9)

According to Jesus, not everything in the Old Testament represents the original intention of the Creator. There were, for instance, many examples of polygamy in the Hebrew Bible, even among prominent Israelites like Abraham or David. King Solomon had 1,000 concubines (that is, mistresses of a lesser status than wives). While such practices were the norm for elite men across global cultures, they are the exception in Scripture and are presented consistently as cautionary tales of strife and exploitation. Here in the New Testament, Jesus tells his hearers that some Old Testament practices—indeed some Old Testament *legislation*—were non-ideal. It was a concession to human stubbornness—"hardness of heart", as he puts it. But in his coming, Jesus has restored things to the original pattern as taught in Genesis 1 and 2: marriage is between one man and one woman for life. Divorce is allowed only for rare exceptions.

According to Jesus, then, sex has two possible meanings. Within marriage, sex is your body's way of (re-)making wedding vows: "till death us do part". Outside of marriage, sex is taking a sledgehammer to a union forged by God himself. Here is an incredibly high (or some might say, "narrow") view of sex. How do Jesus' followers respond?

> *"The disciples said to him, 'If this is the situation*
> *between a husband and wife, it is better not to marry.'"*
>
> *(Matthew 19:10)*

Jesus was followed by red-blooded men, including fishermen like Peter (who was married). But when these men heard that the marital doors were locked with no one getting out alive, they were horrified. Those who were married wished themselves unmarried. (We are not told how Peter's wife reacted when she heard about her husband's response here!) Those who were unmarried began backtracking on any matrimonial plans. This teaching is a strict curtailing of male sexual behaviour.

If we don't notice the strangeness of this view, it might be because we're unaware of what male sexual behaviour is like in the wild. Here's Joseph Henrich comparing us to other animals:

> *"From among our closest evolutionary relatives—apes*
> *and monkeys—guess how many species both live*
> *in large groups, like Homo sapiens, and have only*
> *monogamous pair-bonding? That's right, zero."*[51]

Marriage, the way we do it, is not natural. It's weird. And within human societies monogamy is almost as rare. But if marriage proves too much of a commitment, Jesus offers an alternative (but only one): *Live like a eunuch.*

---

51 Joseph Henrich, *The Weirdest People in the World* (Penguin, 2020), p 258.

> "Jesus replied, 'Not everyone can accept this word, but only those to whom it has been given. For there are eunuchs who were born that way, and there are eunuchs who have been made eunuchs by others—and there are those who choose to live like eunuchs for the sake of the kingdom of heaven. The one who can accept this should accept it.'" (Matthew 19:11-12)

A eunuch was a man without testicles, often forcibly castrated as a slave so as not to be a threat to the master's wives. Jesus says that those who do not embrace marriage can instead embrace this other calling: they can forsake sex altogether and serve undistractedly in the kingdom of God. Those are the options: lifelong monogamy or chaste singleness. There is no third option. As Kyle Harper puts it, in the original sexual revolution "all the world's diffuse erotic energy was to be cramped into one, frail, sacred union."[52]

Henrich calls this teaching the church's "Marriage and Family Program" (MFP). And its effects have been profound. Henrich identifies it as the biggest single contributor to the West's weird psychology and remarkable prosperity. In cultures where high-status men call the shots, they take all the women. This is terrible for the women and for the other men. The Marriage and Family Program redistributes sex and marriage across the sexes and across the classes. In theory anyone can find a mate (a difficult job if Solomon has all the women). This, in Henrich's analysis, "suppresses male-male reproductive competition" and "drains the ... pool

---

52 Kyle Harper, *Shame to Sin* (Harvard University Press, 2016), p 163.

of unmarried men"[53]—a dangerous pool, full of self-styled "involuntary celibates", high on testosterone and low on responsibility. The MFP drastically reduces that pool and instead ties men to their women and their children—their sexual choices and the consequences of those choices. As men are bound to family life this acts naturally as a "testosterone suppression system", lowering the aggression of the male population. Henrich summarizes the effects of the MFP in terms reminiscent of Jesus' "eunuch" language: "The church, through the institution of monogamous marriage, reached down and grabbed men by the testicles."[54]

A HIGHER VIEW

Henrich's analysis is correct as regards the Marriage and Family Program. But questions remain. How did the church "reach down" to people when it did not occupy any cultural heights, certainly not for the first three centuries? Why did dominant men allow themselves to be so restricted? And how do we account for the "live like eunuchs" part of Christ's teaching? Henrich focuses on marriage and family. But Christ holds chaste singleness in even higher regard. In evolutionary terms, such singleness is a dead end. But Christians looked beyond biological realities to spiritual ones:

> "Do you not know that your bodies are temples of the Holy Spirit, who is in you?" (1 Corinthians 6:19)

The apostle Paul here speaks in breathtaking terms

---

53 Joseph Henrich, *The Weirdest People in the World* (Penguin, 2020), p 267.

54 As above, p 273.

about the dignity afforded to human bodies. In the ancient world, many bodies were considered like urinals. In the modern world, we may think of our bodies as playgrounds. But to imagine that our frail human bodies could be homes for God is to imbue the physical with incredible spiritual significance. When such sacred bodies come together, Paul reveals the very highest truth about marriage imaginable:

> "Husbands, love your wives, just as Christ loved the church and gave himself up for her ... 'For this reason a man will leave his father and mother and be united to his wife, and the two will become one flesh.' This is a profound mystery—but I am talking about Christ and the church." (Ephesians 5:25, 31-32)

For Paul, the joining of a man and a woman in marriage points to something beyond it: the love story between Christ and his people. Just as Jesus has loved us and joined himself to us, so husbands and wives are to be joined together as a picture of this divine romance. Marital love is a proclamation of the most profound union.

For this reason, sex within marriage is heartily encouraged:

> "Do not deprive each other except perhaps by mutual consent and for a time, so that you may devote yourselves to prayer. Then come together again."
> (1 Corinthians 7:5)

Notice the stunning idea of mutual consent brought into the bedroom. Such mutuality really did cut both ways. In the previous verse Paul begins by teaching something that would have gained easy assent in the ancient world:

"The wife does not have authority over her own body but yields it to her husband." (v 4)

No one in Paul's day would have objected to this. But the next phrase represents a radical shift in the understanding of sex, marriage, men, women, bodies and choice:

"In the same way, the husband does not have authority over his own body but yields it to his wife."

(1 Corinthians 7:4)

The words "in the same way" represent a revolution. Paul is insisting on complete mutuality. The married couple are to belong to one another as equals. It's hard for us to appreciate how stunning this was. Today we take such mutual consent and commitment for granted. But we take it for granted now because it was radical then.

In the ancient world, the gods were violent rapists, sexual agency was solely in the hands of powerful men, and sexual misbehaviour consisted in the violation of reputations, not of bodies or wills. Into this world came the Christian revolution, where sex is painted on the canvas of divine romance and where two equals unite in a sacred and unbreakable bond. It might be true that the Marriage and Family Program ended up "grabbing testicles" (to use Henrich's phrase), but it could do so only because first it captured hearts.

SLAVES, WOMEN AND CHILDREN
Unsurprisingly the hearts captured by the Jesus movement were initially those most bruised by the

brutalities of the day. In the 2nd century, Celsus (a critic of Christianity whom we have already met) wrote that Christians "are able to convince only the foolish, dishonourable, and stupid, only slaves, women, and little children".[55] Yet what represented a sneer for Celsus was a boast for the early church. Historian Rodney Stark has wondered aloud "why *every* woman who heard about [Christianity] didn't become a Christian."[56] The church became a place of dignity, protection and provision for women. In 251 a bishop in Rome wrote to another in Antioch, pointing out that "more than fifteen hundred widows and distressed persons" were in the care of the local congregation (a congregation of about 30,000). Moderns look back on these congregations as "mini welfare states", but at the time the churches saw themselves as families. In the cosmic romance, those who consent to the committed love of Christ are united, marriage-like, to God's Son. They are thereby brought into the Father's household, calling on fellow Christians as brother and sister. In other words: they are family.

"In Christ Jesus you are all children of God through faith, for all of you who were baptised into Christ have clothed yourselves with Christ. There is neither Jew nor Gentile, neither slave nor free, nor is there male and female, for you are all one in Christ Jesus."

(Galatians 3:26-28)

---

55 From Origen, *Contra Celsum*, Book 3, Chapter 44, quoted in Michael J. Kruger, *Christianity at the Crossroads* (IVP Academic, 2018), p 34-35.

56 Rodney Stark in "Jesus the Game Changer Season One - Rodney Stark Extended Interview". https://youtu.be/3h2OnGUU1Uk, 7:00. Accessed 30th October 2021.

Within the church none are "lords" except Christ, and all are one. Regardless of race, rank or gender, all belong to the family of God. And as family, the beating heart of the church's ethic is love—a trait that floods the New Testament and early Christian writing, yet is barely mentioned in the classical virtue lists. Philosophers such as Plato or Cicero considered the foundational virtues to be wisdom, justice, courage, and moderation—traits well suited to the army barracks. In fact, the word "virtue" is closely related to the word "virile". Both come from the Latin word *vir*, meaning "man". Virtue was "manliness".

But Christ revealed a different kind of God and a different kind of man. He taught that the highest good was to love—to love God and neighbour, and even to love our enemies. And what is love? Paul penned one of the Bible's—indeed literature's—most famous passages:

> *"Love is patient. Love is kind. It does not envy, it does not boast, it is not proud. It does not dishonour others, it is not self-seeking, it is not easily angered, it keeps no record of wrongs." (1 Corinthians 13:4-5)*

These are not the slogans of the drill sergeant but the atmosphere of the healthy family home. And so, to bring this chapter full circle, we should consider one particular aspect of the church's family life: its treatment of children.

In the ancient world sex with boys and girls was not merely tolerated; it was celebrated by writers like Juvenal, Petronius, Horace, Strato, Lucian, and Philostratus.[57] The

---

57   Larry Hurtado, *Destroyer of the Gods* (Baylor University Press, 2017), p 167.

word they used was *pederasty*: love of children. Christians were uniformly disgusted by the practice and called it by a different name—*paidophthoros*: destruction of children.[58] What the classical world called love, Christians called abuse, "thereby construing all sexual contact with the young as an act of corruption".[59] In the reign of the Christian emperor Justinian (527–565), pederasty was outlawed and could be prosecuted well after the abuse took place.[60] Here church and state—preaching and legislation—worked together as a one-two punch against the sexualisation of children.

Today, as "children of the revolution", we take for granted this revolution in our regard for children. The evil of child sexual abuse represents perhaps *the* moral certainty of our day. But our day needs setting in historical context. We view things on *this* side of the Jesus movement: "the single greatest breakthrough against child abuse".[61] Before and without Jesus, it is not always clear to people "what a little girl is worth".

CROOKED LINES ARE CROOKED

Towards the end of Rachael Denhollander's victim-impact statement, she addressed Larry Nassar directly:

> *"In our early hearings, you brought your Bible into the courtroom and you have spoken of praying for forgiveness..."*

---

58 As above, p 167.

59 Kyle Harper, *From Shame to Sin* (Harvard University Press, 2016), p 98.

60 As above, p 13.

61 Paul Offit, *Bad Faith* (Basic Books, 2015), p 127.

As she is a Christian, we might have expected Denhollander to downplay or deny Nassar's professed faith. No one wants to claim the paedophile for their "side". But it's vital to grapple with this reality: those who claim a Christian identity have been among the worst abusers on the planet. Denhollander does not hide from this truth. All Christians acknowledge it is possible to claim the label and deny the transforming reality. As Jesus taught, we must watch out for vicious predators who masquerade as innocent believers: "wolves in sheep's clothing" (Matthew 7:15). But what Denhollander does is less about questioning Nassar's Christianity (though that is certainly appropriate too). Denhollander *applies* his avowed Christianity. She holds him to the standards he professes and the result is a blistering denunciation:

> *"The Bible you carry says it is better for a stone to be [hung] around your neck and you thrown into a lake than for you to make even one child stumble. And you have damaged hundreds."*

The words are from Jesus (Matthew 18:6), whose teaching birthed a revolution in the way children are regarded. Little girls and boys are worth everything. Jesus has taught us this. And, grotesquely, abusers like Nassar have taught us it too—though in photo-negative. The horror of his crime is a testament to the worth of his victims. It's also a testament to the values we hold dear. Denhollander put it like this:

> *"Throughout this process, I have clung to a quote by C.S. Lewis, where he says, 'My argument against God was that the universe seems so cruel and unjust. But how*

*did I get this idea of just, unjust? A man does not call
a line crooked unless he first has some idea of straight.
What was I comparing the universe to when I called it
unjust?'*

"*Larry, I can call what you did evil and wicked because
it was. And I know it was evil and wicked because the
straight line exists. The straight line is not measured
based on your perception or anyone else's perception,
and this means I can speak the truth about my abuse
without minimization or mitigation. And I can call it
evil because I know what goodness is.*"

After the horrors Rachael Denhollander has endured, we
might expect her faith in God to be weakened. Instead
Denhollander has pressed more deeply into that sense
of injustice. It was the same for the author she cited:
C.S. Lewis. In recognising the crookedness of this world,
Lewis and Denhollander are pointing us to the straight
line. If there was no such thing as a straight line, there
would be no such thing as a crooked line either. Lines
would simply be lines, and stuff would simply happen.
But we know crooked when we see it. And we know evil
when we see it.

Denhollander is able to call Nassar's acts evil. That does not
mean unforgivable. She offered her abuser forgiveness in
this same statement—a remarkably Christian action. But
she extended forgiveness *because* the abuse was wrong:
not just unpleasant or painful or culturally inappropriate.
It was hellishly wrong. Wrong with a capital W. Yet if
it really was Wrong, says Denhollander, then there is
something that is Right with a capital R.

All this forces us to consider the standards by which we judge abuse. For abuse to be abuse we have to believe certain things: that bodies should be treated as temples; that sex is sacred; that children are valuable; and that the powerful should not exploit the weak but serve them. These values constitute the straight line against which we judge Nassar's actions as crooked. But such values are by no means universal. They are not the way that the animal kingdom operates, and they are not the presumptions of other human societies. They are Christian beliefs. Larry Nassar is not excused of his evils by claiming some kind of Christianity; he is accused by it. It is, very particularly, the goodness of Jesus that defines the evil of his abuse.

Sometimes we only realise what is important to us when it's threatened. And sometimes, tragically, it takes the violation of persons, of bodies, and of consent, to show us that these have been sacred values all along. But listen to your own heartfelt response when Denhollander asks, "What is a little girl worth?" You do not answer that question scientifically or economically. Nor do you answer it merely sociologically or psychologically. The deepest and truest answer to that question is a spiritual one. And when a guttural "Everything" rises up within you, that's your Christianity talking.

5. ENLIGHTENMENT

"It really is medieval; for this day and age it's shocking."[62]

— New Zealand resident complaining about
cell-phone coverage, 2018

You know "medieval" has become a toxic brand when even patchy mobile phone reception is slapped with the label. Technically, "medieval" is the historical period between the fall of Rome (410) and rise of the Renaissance (14th–15th centuries), also known as the Middle Ages. But these days, the word is synonymous with "backwards", "broken" or "brutal". A quick online search reveals that "medieval" can also describe computer systems,[63] the Taliban,[64] a defensive style of rugby,[65] a salacious TV show,[66] and the psychological

---

62 Residents frustrated at 'medieval' cellphone coverage in the Far North, Stuff website, https://www.stuff.co.nz/auckland/local-news/northland/106654790/residents-frustrated-at-medieval-cellphone-coverage-in-the-far-north. Accessed 3rd November 2021.

63 "They're using a computer system that seems positively medieval by today's standards." Suggested example of "medieval" in a sentence, *Merriam-Webster Dictionary*. https://www.merriam-webster.com/dictionary/medieval. Accessed 28th October 2021.

64 "Taliban Give The Word Medieval A Bad Name", Douglas Murray, *The Sun*, 13th July 2021 https://www.thesun.co.uk/news/15586446/douglas-murray-taliban-government. Accessed 28th October 2021.

65 Twitter, @kgoatlapa, 26th July 2014. https://twitter.com/kgoatlapa/status/492963576995672065

66 "How amoral Love Island is taking us back to the Dark Ages", Sarah Vine, *Daily Mail*, 22nd August 2021. https://www.dailymail.co.uk/debate/article-9915397/SARAH-

torment of football penalty shoot outs.[67]

The word has become so detached from history that no one notices how ridiculous it is to call computers, cell phones and TV shows "medieval". The word no longer means a historical period, really. It just means awful. Or cruel. Or outdated. It probably also implies violence and torture, as with the *Pulp Fiction* character Marsellus Wallace, who threatens to "get medieval" on his enemies.

Here, then, is your warning. In this chapter we are about to get medieval. But not in the *Pulp Fiction* sense. Actually, as we'll see, getting medieval can be truly enlightening. But we might have to overturn some powerful prejudices about the Middle Ages. Certainly I have had to overcome many of my own. When I think of the Middle Ages, I first imagine battles, boils and bubonic plague. That is, at best, a lopsided assessment of the age that brought us universities, Magna Carta, and Chartres Cathedral. So what has happened to our appreciation of the past? Why do we find it so easy to "throw shade" at the medieval period?

"Throwing shade" is modern slang for an insult, but it's the perfect description of what we've been doing for centuries. Long after historians stopped the practice, most of us continue to call the Middle Ages the "dark ages". We look back on it as "benighted", and we see

VINE-amoral-Love-Island-taking-Dark-Ages.html. Accessed 3rd November 2021.

67 "Love, courage and solidarity: 20 essential lessons young athletes taught us this summer", Sirin Kale, *The Guardian*. 5 August 2021. https://www.theguardian.com/sport/2021/aug/05/20-essential-lessons-young-athletes-taught-us-this-summer-euros-olympics. Accessed 3rd November 2021.

ourselves as "enlightened". Both those outlooks are totally instinctive now. But, as this chapter will show, such views have developed for profoundly Christian reasons. We will learn much about history in this chapter as we bust the myth of the "dark ages" but, more than that, we will learn about ourselves—about the ways we have been shaped by Christianity, even as we critique it.

A HISTORY OF THROWING SHADE

Imagine a world without Christianity. There's an episode of the animation *Family Guy* which does just that. In "Road to the Multiverse" Stewie and Brian discover a remote control able to zap you into alternate realities. At one point they access an incredibly advanced parallel universe. Even though it's the same town in the same year, people can levitate, there's speed-of-light rail travel, and every disease can be cured instantly. The explanation?

"In this [parallel] universe, Christianity never existed, which means the dark ages of scientific repression never occurred, and thus humanity is a thousand years more advanced."[68]

Family Guy is not alone in running such a thought experiment. Many have wondered how civilisation might have progressed if the church had not mired us in a thousand-year "dark age". The conclusion seems to be that we'd be much better off. Where does such thinking come from?

---

68 Stewie, *Family Guy*, season 8, episode 1, 2009. https://tvshowtranscripts.ourboard. org/viewtopic.php?f=430&t=21253. Accessed 28th October 2021.

Famously Carl Sagan (1934–1996), a great populariser of science, called the years from the 5th to the 15th century, "a millennium gap". This was, thought Sagan, "a poignant lost opportunity for the human species". For his groundbreaking TV series *Cosmos*, he even provided a timeline packed with names and discoveries prior to 400 and resuming service again post-1400. The intervening centuries contained no entries whatsoever—a "dark ages" indeed. Where did Sagan get the idea?

The notion of a lost "dark ages" was promoted most especially during the so-called "Age of Enlightenment". The Enlightenment (17th and 18th centuries) featured thinkers like Immanuel Kant, Edward Gibbon, John Locke, David Hume and Jean Jacques Rousseau. Their telling of history (and this is, I'll admit, a generalisation) cast Christianity as a regressive force, suppressing the glories of the classical world for a thousand years until a number of brave heroes rescued us from the clutches of Popes, monks and Inquisitors. First came the Renaissance of the 14th and 15th centuries, which saw a rediscovery of classical learning. Then the scientists of the 16th and 17th centuries came along to finish off faith, leaving the way clear for an age of reason.

The Age of Reason was the title of Thomas Paine's famous book in which he contrasted the rationality of his time with an earlier "age of faith". For Paine, "faith" was equated with superstition and ignorance:

> "The age of ignorance commenced with the Christian system ... [It was a] long interregnum [i.e. interval] of science ... a vast chasm of many hundred years ... a vast

sandy desert, in which not a shrub appears to intercept the vision to the fertile hills beyond."[69]

Paine felt the way we all tend to feel (nowadays at least). We reckon that *we are the ones we've been waiting for.* We view history as merely the backstory for our own grand entrance. Paine was just a bit bolder in saying this. He and his cohort claimed to be on the fertile hills, looking back at the barren wasteland. They were enlightened and reasonable, and their forebears were ignorant faithheads. This is the view we have inherited in the modern West. We find ourselves standing with Thomas Paine, looking back on the "vast, sandy desert" with a sense of superiority. Certainly, those are my instincts. I've been throwing shade at the Middle Ages all my life (sometimes in print, if you can find it!).

But this chapter is about two things. Firstly, we will identify the enlightenment that already existed in the "dark ages". The medieval period saw great advances in education, philosophy, theology, law, politics, literature, art, music, architecture, commerce and technology. Furthermore, the period laid crucial foundations for the developments which this book will soon consider: science, freedom and progress. In terms of the "enlightenment" which this chapter explores, there was, in these centuries, a mixed but nevertheless remarkable commitment to education and persuasion as the means of spreading "the light of Christ".

---

69   Thomas Paine, *The Age of Reason*, Part I, Chapter XII. From *The Writings of Thomas Paine: Volume IV*, ed. Moncure Daniel Conway (Project Gutenberg, 2001).

So, on the one hand, we will point to the light already present in those centuries but, secondly, we will press into *why* we have been throwing shade at the Middle Ages for so long. Where does our sense of historical superiority come from? The answer might surprise us.

Before that, though, we need to catch up on the timeline.

FROM CULT TO CULTURE

How did the obscure, marginal Jesus movement of the 1st century become the dominant religious force in the Western world in a few centuries? That is the question posed by the subtitle of sociologist Rodney Stark's *The Rise of Christianity*. In the book he points to many factors including conversions, birth rates, the role of women, charity, martyrs and even pandemics. He has estimated that from the time of the first Easter, the church began growing at a rate of 40% per decade (a modest but relentless 3.4% per year). By the year 300, Christians numbered perhaps 6 million: about a tenth of the empire. When the Emperor Constantine converted to Christianity in 312, he was backing a winning horse. As Stark writes, "Constantine's conversion would better be seen as a response to the massive exponential wave in progress, not as its cause".[70]

In 313 Constantine's "Edict of Milan" granted freedoms to Christians that were remarkable for the time and a model of religious toleration for the coming centuries.

---

70 Rodney Stark, *The Rise of Christianity: How the Obscure, Marginal Jesus Movement Became the Dominant Religious Force in the Western World in a Few Centuries* (HarperSanFrancisco, 1997), p 10.

This was sweet relief to a Christian community that had suffered severe persecutions, especially around the turn of the 4th century. But now the tide was turning, and by 380, when the Emperor Theodosius made Christianity Rome's official religion, more than half the population had already converted. In a few short centuries Christianity had gone from radical counterculture to dominant cultural power. This was an extraordinary shift in the church's relationship with the world.

And then, in 410, the world itself changed, violently.

FALL AND RISE

When people speak of the fall of the Roman Empire, they usually mean in the 5th century when the western half fell. But there was also an eastern half, known as the Byzantine Empire (with its capital in what is modern-day Istanbul). It lasted a thousand years beyond its western counterpart, though it would suffer much through Muslim invasions from the 7th century onwards.

The west, though, fell with a crash. In 410 the Visigoths (Germanic tribes) sacked Rome. This was an inconceivable shock to those living within the empire's reach. Rome had been considered "the eternal city" and the *pax Romana* (the peace of Rome) had provided centuries-long political stability. With those certainties smashed and the empire splintering into hundreds of independent mini-states, there needed to be a higher vision—something beyond merely human securities. The church provided such a vision. And one thinker in particular helped the west to face the unthinkable.

Augustine, the north African bishop (354–430), penned 5 million words of philosophical, theological, legal and other writings, none more influential than his towering *City of God*. In it he distinguished between the fragile earthly realm and the eternal heavenly kingdom. Rome, a city of man, might fall, but the city of God—expressed in the community of the church—was forever. This distinction was vital (and novel when you consider how emperors had been worshipped for centuries), and it gave rise to the concept of "the secular realm". "Secular" means "this age", which Augustine contrasted with the eternal "sacred realm". By the time of the 11th and 12th centuries, the biblical concept of "the secular", which Augustine had planted, attained "a spectacular bloom", as Tom Holland has called it.[71] What we have come to think of as "the separation of church and state" sprung up in the supposedly "sandy desert" of the Middle Ages.

But while most of us today are attracted to the "secular" side of the distinction, those reeling from the fall of Rome found solace in the sacred. In uncertain times, many pagan peoples desired the church's sense of security. Around the year 500, the king of the Franks (in western Europe) converted, and for centuries the succeeding Merovingian (c. 500–750) and Carolingian kingdoms (750–887) remained officially Christian.

While some from pagan lands were turning to the church, the church for its part was sending emissaries— missionaries—to the nations. But the way the church sought to spread its influence would become a question

---

71 Tom Holland, *Dominion* (Little, Brown, 2019), p 214.

that would take many centuries (and many failures) to settle. In the past, empires sought to spread their influence almost always by force. The Persians had a vision for how surrounding nations needed to reject "the lie" and turn to the "light". The Romans had a "peace"— the *pax Romana*—which they sought to share with the barbarians beyond. But their *means* of spreading such influence involved the sword, or the threat of the sword. How would the rule of *Christ* be extended?

THREAT OR PERSUASION?

Christianity has been a missionary faith from the beginning. Christ himself was the light (John 8:12), and he came to dispel *the night before Christmas*. The church, then, was commissioned to continue this enlightening work. Christ called Christians "the light of the world" (Matthew 5:14). They are his "witnesses ... to the ends of the earth" (Acts 1:8). As annoying as others may find it, Christians cannot keep themselves to themselves, nor can they say of those outside the faith, "Each to their own". Christians deeply desire to enlighten others. And so it was for this reason that, in 597, Pope Gregory the Great sent Augustine (a different Augustine) to Britain to convert the Anglo-Saxons.

Augustine was commanded by Gregory to use only "gentle means". His goal was persuasion. His method was teaching and preaching. And he was successful, converting King Aethelbert of Kent and becoming the first Archbishop of Canterbury. This was a precedent for so much of the way the church in the west sought to shine its light on those pagan nations it considered shrouded in darkness.

A century on and Britain was not simply receiving missionaries; it was sending them. Boniface (675–754), from Devon, in the Saxon kingdom of Wessex, was sent by Pope Gregory II to share the light of Christ with the Saxons in Germanic lands. In the words of his advisor, the Bishop of Winchester, his goal was "to convince them by many documents and arguments".[72] This mission of persuasion and education was largely successful, as he planted churches and religious communities throughout what we now call Germany. Yet in 754 he visited hostile lands and was hacked to death by those he had been seeking to reach.

In advancing Christ's kingdom, Boniface kept to a policy of non-violence and non-retaliation, even to the point of death. The sword he used was emphatically not the sword of violence but what the apostle Paul had called "the sword of the Spirit, which is the word of God" (Ephesians 6:17). Non-violence and word-based persuasion are vitally linked in Christian theology and in the examples of such missionaries. Tom Holland summarises the lesson we learn from Boniface: "to convert was to *educate*".[73]

In the following century this lesson was sorely needed by the Frankish king Charles the Great, aka Charlemagne (742–814). Though he considered himself loyal to the church, his sword was very much of the steel variety. He wielded it ruthlessly, expanding his Carolingian kingdom to dominate most of western Europe until, in 800, it became the "Holy Roman Empire" with himself as "Augustus"—a new Caesar.

72   John Dickson, *Bullies and Saints* (Zondervan, 2021), p 144.

73   Tom Holland, *Dominion* (Little, Brown, 2019), p 206, emphasis added.

Charlemagne's path to power was a brutal one. When the Saxons stood in his way, Charlemagne beheaded 4,500 of them in a single day. Three years later, in 785, he finally brought them to heel and imposed what amounted to a policy of baptism or death. This was, in the words of one modern writer, "Charlemagne's Jihad".[74] There is, then, real darkness in these ages. There are concrete reasons why "getting medieval" might be associated today with brutality.

But we don't have to wait until the Age of Enlightenment before Charlemagne's behaviour is called out. One of his contemporaries, Alcuin of York (735–804), was bold enough to write to Charlemagne directly with his criticism. "A person can be drawn into the faith, not forced into it," wrote Alcuin. We must follow "the example of the Apostles: let them be preachers, not plunderers".[75] For "faith arises from the will, not from compulsion".[76] Alcuin was reflecting the way of Christ, the wisdom of the Scriptures, the example of the early church, and the teaching of missionary bishops like Gregory, who, two centuries before, had urged Augustine to use "gentle means". Charlemagne was violently out of step with the Spirit of Jesus.

The church's official teaching would later agree with Alcuin's position. In the 12th century all "harsh means" were forbidden since faith arises from the will, not compulsion. Enlightenment comes through education

---

74 Yitzhak Hen, quoted in John Dickson, *Bullies and Saints* (Zondervan, 2021), p 150.

75 John Dickson, *Bullies and Saints* (Zondervan, 2021), p 152.

76 Tom Holland, *Dominion* (Little, Brown, 2019), p 209.

and persuasion. Charlemagne's violence therefore proved
the exception, not the rule.

At this point I can hear a couple of objections: what about
the Crusades and the Spanish Inquisition? These are
commonly raised when discussing Christianity generally
and the Middle Ages particularly, and no wonder. They
are stark examples of the church using "harsh means".
Perhaps these atrocities demonstrate that Christianity
is comfortable with violence and coercion—maybe even
founded upon it. We will briefly address both topics using
the ideas of the "crooked and straight lines" discussed
last chapter. Essentially we will 1) bust the myths, 2) own
what's crooked, and 3) insist on the straight line.

HANG ON: WHAT ABOUT THE CRUSADES?

Bust the Myths

There are different ways of telling the story of the Crusades
(1096–1229). Try this on for size: the Crusades were five
waves of campaigns (or six, depending on how you count
them) launched to recapture Muslim-held Jerusalem for
Christendom. Islam had spread, unapologetically, by wars
of conquest since its inception and had held Jerusalem
since 637. After four and a half centuries of losses, the
Byzantine emperor pleaded for help from Christians in
western Europe against a resurgent Muslim foe about to
wipe the entire eastern empire off the map. Pope Urban II
responded, as did tens of thousands of Crusaders. Their
surprising victory in the first campaign, recapturing
Jerusalem against the odds, was costly for all involved
and gave way to many subsequent failures. Until the last
century or so, this is the way Muslims themselves saw

the Crusades: as a largely embarrassing failure for the Christians.

The historian Rodney Stark summarises his view like this: "The Crusades were not unprovoked. They were not the first round of European colonialism. They were not conducted for land, loot, or converts. The Crusaders were not barbarians who victimized the cultivated Muslims. The Crusades are not a blot on the history of Christianity. No apologies are required."[77] This is *one* way to tell the story and it certainly involves some important myth-busting. But another historian (and Christian), John Dickson, has a different take. He asks us to stare the "crookedness" of the Crusades full in the face.

Own What's Crooked

Dickson argues that the Crusades "stand as a symbol ... of the church's all-too-human capacity for dogma, hatred, and violence toward enemies. Admitting this reality should be instinctive for genuine Christians." He writes of atrocities committed on the way to Jerusalem and includes this eye-witness account of 15 July 1099, the day the Crusaders breached the Muslim defences:

"Wonderful sights were to be seen. Some of our men cut off the heads of their enemies; others shot them with arrows, so that they fell from towers; others tortured them longer by casting them into the flames. Piles of heads, hands and feet were to be seen in the streets of the city ... It was a just and splendid judgement of God."[78]

---

77 Rodney Stark, *The Triumph of Christianity* (Bravo Ltd, 2012), p 234.

78 Quoted in John Dickson, *Bullies and Saints* (Zondervan, 2021), p 3.

It is this mixing of God and torture that we find so abhorrent, and yet it was central to the Crusades. Central too was a mixing of church and state which we now find so problematic. It was popes who recruited and sent the soldiers. It was leading theologians of the day, like Bernard of Clairvaux (1090–1153), who assured them, "Take the sign of the cross, and you shall gain pardon for every sin". It was the sign of the cross which the soldiers wore on their uniforms even as they inverted its meaning. The Crusades were appallingly crooked. But once again we must ask, crooked when judged against what?

Insist on the Straight Line

The straight line which condemns the Crusades is precisely the sign under which they fought: the cross. The name "Crusader" derives from the Latin for cross (crux) and means "one marked by the cross". The common way to refer to a Crusader journeying to Jerusalem was to say they were "taking up their cross". This was a deliberate echo of Christ's own command: "Whoever wants to be my disciple must deny themselves and take up their cross and follow me" (Matthew 16:24). On *Jesus'* lips, this meant to bear suffering. For the Crusaders it meant to inflict it.

The contradiction was grotesque but not all were blind to it. During the fifth Crusade, for instance, Francis of Assisi (1181–1226) travelled to the battlefield (at this point in Egypt) and tried to dissuade the soldiers from violence and persuade them of persuasion instead. (He wasn't persuasive, ironically.) He then requested to be allowed to preach to the sultan of Egypt—an incredible request which, even more incredibly, was granted. When the missionary encounter happened, neither side was convinced by the other, yet somehow Francis escaped with his head intact. Through it all, his embrace of non-violence and persuasion at the risk of his life was suggestive of what true "cross bearing" looks like.

The comparison is stark, but it's worth pressing into: when fought under the banner of the cross, what can we call the Crusades except a foul contradiction? But now judge them by a different standard: if such battles were fought under the banner of an Alexander the Great, or a Julius Caesar, or even a Muhammad, what would we call them? In that case they are unexceptional, standard practice: business as usual. If we are outraged by the Crusades—and we should be—that is *Christian* outrage we're experiencing.

HANG ON: WHAT ABOUT THE SPANISH INQUISITION?

Bust the Myths

The Spanish Inquisition (1478–1834) was a tribunal set up to investigate and prosecute charges of heresy within Spain and her colonies. The Inquisition became infamous for its brutality—with Protestants historically having led the way in the myth-making: reporting or intimating greatly inflated numbers of deaths.

However, sober-minded historical research (and there are very careful records to consult) puts the death toll at about 2,000 executions for the notorious 50 years under Tomas de Torquemada and his protégés (1480–1530). In the following 300 years there were a further 3,000 executions. Compare even the worst of Torquemada's time with the last 45 years of state executions in the USA and the levels are about the same. More soberingly, we could compare it with the Reign of Terror in revolutionary France during the "Age of Enlightenment." In the nine months following the storming of the Bastille (1789), 17,000 were executed in the name of liberty, equality and fraternity. Or compare it with the Red Terror following the Russian Revolution (1917), in which "the best estimates set the probable number of executions at about a hundred thousand."[79] This is an execution rate 1,400 times that of the Spanish Inquisition. Having said all that...

Own What's Crooked

These 5,000 deaths are a dark stain on the history of the church. Each one is a sin against the person killed as well as a crime against "freedom of conscience". Persuasion, not power, ought to be the means by which influence is spread, and every death in the name of Christianity is an assault on that principle. It is truly dark. But then, why do we recoil so instinctively from such an imposition of force? Once again, the crooked line testifies to the straight...

Insist on the Straight Line

It is wrong to impose your views on others—whether the views you prize involve Christianity or freedom, democracy, the worker's paradise or a Muslim caliphate. But this is wrong because we have a sense of what is right. We believe that there is a fundamental difference between words and violence. We believe that force is

---

79 Lincoln, W. Bruce, *Red Victory: A History of the Russian Civil War* (Simon & Schuster, 1989), p 384.

not the way to extend your influence, but persuasion is. Where did we get these notions? It's Jesus who taught us to "put away your sword" (Matthew 26:52, NLT), and it's Paul who, instead, urged Christians to use "the sword of the Spirit, which is the word of God" (Ephesians 6:17). Wickedly, the Inquisition used harsh means to bring about coercion. But if we believe instead in gentle means, it's the unique foundations of Christianity which will give best support.

LIGHT IN THE DARKNESS

Should we spread our influence by violence or by persuasion? By coercion or by conversation? By force or by faith? At the beginning of the 780s, Charlemagne and Alcuin represented two radically different approaches to that question. Charlemagne was carrying on his imperial mission in the customary way, and the body count was mounting. But incredibly, by the end of the 780s, Alcuin, the scholar, had changed the mind of Charlemagne, the warlord. He persuaded him about persuasion. Charlemagne backtracked on his forced-conversions policy and—never one to do anything by halves—threw himself into a new venture. The man who would be crowned "Augustus" became an educationalist.

If persuasion was the true "weapon" of the Christian ruler, then Charlemagne needed to deploy Alcuin and his fellow scholars so that armies of new learners might be raised up. This is what he did, with zeal. "Without education they were doomed; without education, they could not be brought to Christ."[80] And so in 789 Charlemagne established major educational reforms which proved to be the beginning of what's been called the Carolingian Renaissance. Over 70 schools were established. These taught the liberal arts—a foundation of grammar, logic, and rhetoric followed by arithmetic, geometry, music and astronomy. From there, some could opt for medicine or law or theology, but notice the breadth of learning expected at the outset.

Notice too the sources of such learning. They were not limited to Scripture or even to Christian authors. They included "Plato, Aristotle, Galen, Pliny the Elder, Horace, Cicero, Seneca, Virgil, Livy, Ovid, and about sixty other authors".[81] In fact, during the 8th and 9th centuries, it has been estimated that perhaps 50,000 books were copied and produced from across this breadth of authors.[82] And the practice only grew. In the 12th century there was a "veritable flood of translations into Latin" of the classical works. The earliest catalogues that survive from the monasteries of the day reveal "extensive holdings of classical authors".[83]

If you have ever heard the charge that Christians destroyed classical learning, overwhelmingly the opposite is the case; they studied and stewarded these ancient works with immense care. These centuries were certainly an age of faith, but that did not mean ignorance, credulity

---

80   Tom Holland, *Dominion* (Little, Brown, 2019), p 211.

81   John Dickson, *Bullies and Saints* (Zondervan, 2021), p 164-5.

82   As above, p 165.

83   Rodney Stark, *The Triumph of Christianity* (Bravo Ltd, 2012), p 251.

or superstition. It meant learning. Those who consider themselves part of the Age of Reason risk casting themselves as a caricature hero to save the world from a caricature villain. But we ought to take stock of the enlightenment which already existed in the Middle Ages. Let me point to five key developments in medieval times: technology, human rights, universities, parliaments and the Reformation.

TECHNOLOGY

Labour-saving innovations were a vital concern in medieval Europe, with the religious communities, like monasteries, leading the way. Where the Romans had relied heavily on slaves (called "living tools" by Aristotle and Plato), monks set about making mechanical ones. To replace the drudgery of human toil there were great advances in wind and water power, in sail technology, and in agronomy (selective plant-breeding, the three-field rotation system, the heavy plough, and more). Eyeglasses were invented—a huge help for an increasingly literate people.

For the praises of God, immense and ornate structures were built: cathedrals (there are 26 in England alone). These were made possible by architectural innovations like flying buttresses and the Gothic arch. They housed the world's most sophisticated machines till then: pipe organs. Soon though, that accolade would belong to mechanical clocks, invented in the 13th century, to some degree to serve the monasteries' need for regular hours of prayer. As far as a medieval Christian was concerned, technology was a place where the good of humanity and the glory of God would embrace.

HUMAN RIGHTS

Earlier we noted Tom Holland's analogy about "the secular realm": Augustine "planted" the concept, and it attained a "spectacular bloom" in the 11th and 12th centuries.[84] These particular centuries are an important but often overlooked flowering in history. They are sometimes called the "Gregorian reforms" after Pope Gregory VII (1020-1085). Others speak of the "papal revolution" since there were multiple popes who carried forward what Gregory dubbed his "reformation". During this period the legal rulings of church courts were being compiled and analysed, taking the assumptions of the faith—notions like equality, charity, marriage, and much more—and codifying them as church laws ("canon law").

What emerged was a robust and unprecedented language of "rights". This was new. From the beginning, Christians had felt obligations (like the obligation to give to the poor), but now church lawyers were enshrining the other side of the equation—*rights*. The wealthy don't just have a responsibility to the poor; the poor have a claim on the wealthy. They have rights—human rights, which are possessed by each person regardless of their position or resources but simply by nature. Over time such notions became part of secular law too. The idea that we are free and equal individuals under law with certain inalienable rights was not an Enlightenment discovery but a biblical truth, planted by Genesis, cultivated by the church and blooming brightly in those dark days of medieval Christendom.

---

84   Tom Holland, *Dominion* (Baker Books, 2019), p 214.

UNIVERSITIES

One of the great gifts of Christian civilisation to the world emerged right in the heart of the Middle Ages. We have seen how learning was prized and pursued in the monasteries, but universities were something new. They differed from the Greek and Roman philosophical schools that were founded by a single teacher or school of thought. They were different too from Chinese academies for training court officials. These bodies existed not to pass down received wisdom or simply to train people in vocational skills. They were established for the pursuit of higher learning. The goal was not just preservation of knowledge but innovation, which was now incentivised since scholars would compete to gain the attention of the different faculties. In the 1200s Bologna, Paris, Oxford and Cambridge all had universities. In the following century another 20 at least were added, with thousands of students attending. Today universities have become universal, but it was sentiments like Oxford's motto that inspired them: "God is my guiding light".

PARLIAMENTS

In these centuries, church lawyers were also busy applying theological concepts to political realities. If citizens were possessors of "rights", then rulers could never be thought to have unlimited powers. Instead, rulers were meant to "minister" to the ruled; that's certainly what Christ taught. And what's more, in the Old Testament God established contracts called "covenants" with his people, in which he pledged to be a good and merciful Ruler. This became a model for how earthly rulers should treat their people too. If they failed to honour the rights of their citizens, they "broke the compact by virtue of which [they were] appointed".[85] All of this sounds very similar to the "social contract theories" espoused by political philosophers of the Enlightenment, but it came about 600 years earlier. And such reforms had practical effects too. In England, for instance, the king's powers began to be limited via Magna Carta (1215). Parliament was established (1275) and extended to commoners (1295, 1327). Legally and politically, reform and revitalization was slowly but surely remaking the world. And then it was the turn of religion itself: the event we usually call *the* Reformation.

THE REFORMATION

Martin Luther (1483–1546) has sometimes been called "the last medieval man and the first modern man". As an Augustinian monk and a university professor he was very much a product of the Middle Ages. But such privileged positions also gave him ready access to the Bible, which he treated with the kind of attention to detail taught him by his monastic and scholastic training. He had felt trapped by a religious system in which he was never free of guilt. He would perform endless exacting penances (penalties enforced by the Roman Catholic church for sins), but he never felt forgiven. Yet when he came upon a statement of Paul's in Romans 1, he made the breakthrough: "I felt that I was altogether born again and had entered paradise itself through open gates".[86]

---

85 Larry Siedentop, *Inventing the Individual: The Origins of Western Liberalism* (Penguin, 2015), p 249.

86 *Luther's Works* 34:337; quoted in Robert Kolb and Charles P. Arand, *The Genius of Luther's Theology* (Baker Publishing, 2008), p 36.

The verses in question were Romans 1:16-17, which say that righteousness—being right with God—is "by faith". This felt like liberation for Luther, who came to see that salvation was not the conditional outcome of a long system of penances, presided over by the institutional church. Instead, salvation was like getting married. It is accomplished the moment the husband and wife unite. And Jesus, like a rich prince, has given himself to a poor prostitute (us). We contribute only our debts (our sins), but he pays our debts (on the cross) and gives us all his riches (his righteousness). Through this marriage-like union, he makes us righteous (declared innocent before God), not for any goodness of our own but simply because we have received him. In other words, we are justified by faith alone.

When Luther maintained his views, conscientiously objecting to both the pope and the emperor, he was radically questioning authority and, at the same time, insisting on his freedom of personal conscience. While elevating the Bible, he was also downgrading tradition and institutional authority. All these values feel very contemporary (aside from the biblical one). This is why Luther is thought of as the first "modern" figure of history. And from him we have inherited a "modern" (and modernizing) view of history.

STEP INTO THE LIGHT

"Always reforming" was a popular Protestant slogan. "After the darkness comes the light" was another. Luther's concern was with a spiritual darkness, and there was certainly plenty of that around. But once these ideas got into the bloodstream of the culture, they began to tilt attitudes towards other things too—including the past. We see it as in constant need of reform and enlightenment. If such views are not balanced by any other considerations, we will start to see our history less as praiseworthy and more as problematic.

And so it is that, in the 17th and 18th centuries, Enlightenment thinkers like Thomas Paine called the Middle Ages a thousand-year darkness that had reigned over the earth. It was a "nighttime" for the world, answered only by Renaissance (an Old French word literally meaning "re-birth"). It was a "vast, sandy desert" which we have now crossed in order to enter the promised land. What do you notice about these views of the past? They are flavoured by something profoundly Christian— more particularly, Protestant. Those who critiqued the "age of faith" of the Middle Ages could not help but be shaped by that faith. And, at the same time, those who trumpeted the value of reason found themselves being less than rational when it came to the church.

It is patently *unreasonable* to call the Middle Ages barren when they contain the glories of medieval cathedrals, the founding of universities, the establishment of parliaments, the poetry of Dante and Geoffrey Chaucer; the list really does go on. While the full structures were not yet in place, the basic intellectual foundations for modern liberal democracies were being laid: the separation of church and state; human rights; theories about just wars, just rulers, just laws and just societies. All this was established by Christian thinkers for Christian reasons, yet Enlightenment sages saw only desert. The *failure* of reason here ought to strike us powerfully. Just ten minutes spent in the cathedral of York Minster (completed in 1472) should dispel the myth of a "dark ages", and yet the myth persists.

Why? We learned it from a medieval monk.

6. SCIENCE

"We are shining the light of science on this invisible killer [coronavirus]
... We will be driven by the science."

— Boris Johnson, 2020

Along with every other world leader, UK prime minister, Boris Johnson, was keen to assure the nation that when it comes to the COVID pandemic, the government would "follow the science", be "guided by the science", or be "driven by the science"—take your pick. And take your pick of what is meant by "the science". It's assumed that we're talking about immunologists, virologists and epidemiologists, but even they disagree. How do we adjudicate?

And might there be other kinds of scientist we want to consult? Might sociologists be relevant guides? Psychologists? Health-care economists? At a stretch, could they be covered by the label "the science"? What about ethicists, political philosophers or historians—ought we to be guided by them? They don't sound very "scientific", so probably not. What about religious leaders?

To modern ears, "religious leaders" sounds like a ridiculous addition to the mix. In a modern democracy, "We will be guided by the priests" is unlikely to fly as a slogan. Yet in previous centuries the priests were prominent in leading the people through times of plague. Over and above vital medical treatments, quarantine, and so on, there was once a sense that our ultimate "leader", "driver" and "guide" was God. Nowadays, it's obvious that science is our guide. And not just science: *the* science. We have the sense that there is a unified thing called "the science" which shines its light, which commands our allegiance, and which will deliver us from evil. And what do you notice about this description? It sounds suspiciously like the traditional role for God.

So has science replaced God? If "the science" is our "light" in dark times—our primary source of comfort and hope—doesn't that crowd out the need for a religious dimension? Perhaps there is a turf war between science and faith. And, let's face it, we have iPhones now, and vaccines and space travel. Faith has lost—spectacularly so.

This is certainly the sense I get when I talk to people about faith. A very common response is "No thanks. I'm more of a scientist." Perhaps that's your own feeling too. Overwhelmingly, the people in my life with no interest in faith are not *anti*-God; they're pro-science, pro-modernity, pro-progress. It's a case of "No hard feelings, but I'm good with science". But—this is the point of the chapter—what if you don't have to choose?

It seems so natural to us that science and faith are at war. But historically that's a novel view. The founders of the modern scientific method would be baffled by the dispute. So what happened?

FRIENDS BECOMING FOES?
When Boris Johnson called science a shining "light", he was using a well-worn analogy. 300 years earlier the

poet Alexander Pope used it of Isaac Newton and his discoveries:

"Nature, and Nature's Laws lay hid in Night:
God said, 'Let Newton be!' and all was light."[87]

This epitaph for the father of modern physics perfectly demonstrates how science and faith were viewed during the so-called "scientific revolution" (16th – 17th century). Here God and Newton are very much on the same team. Science and scientists are a gift of God, and they help to do God's job: dispelling the darkness of ignorance. Then something changed.

Through the Enlightenment of the 18th century, a different understanding developed. By the 19th century, some began speaking of a great conflict between God and science. And for them, the darkness being dispelled was not human ignorance. The light of science was driving out *Christianity*. That was the view of US president Thomas Jefferson, for instance:

"Priests ... dread the advance of science as witches do the
approach of day-light."[88]

For Jefferson, the church represented the forces of night, fighting a losing battle against science. Resistance was futile. To oppose scientific progress would be like shackling the earth, like halting its inexorable turn, like

---

87 *Oxford Essential Quotations (4th ed)*, ed. Susan Ratcliffe (Oxford University Press, 2016). https://www.oxfordreference.com/view/10.1093/acref/9780191826719.001.0001/q-oro-ed4-00007865S. Accessed 19th November 2021.

88 Thomas Jefferson, Letter to José Correia da Serra, 11th April 1820.

extinguishing the sun. But, however hard the church tried to stop it, the light would come, the shadows of ignorance and dogma would be swallowed and the world would be born again.

By the end of the 19th century, the idea of a pitched battle between science and religion had bedded down in the popular imagination. In 1874 John Draper wrote *History of the Conflict Between Religion and Science*. Then the "conflict" was upgraded to full-blown "warfare" by Andrew Dickson, who wrote *A History of the Warfare of Science with Theology* in 1896. Thanks to these polemical works, the belief that science and religion were at war became, in the words of one modern book, "the idea that wouldn't die."[89]

We now have a name for this outlook on science and faith: the "conflict thesis". It's still a prominent view today. But in this chapter, we're going to do something scientific. We will examine the thesis and test it against the facts. What we will find is that the theory is not supported by the evidence. And so, like good scientists, we should revise our hypothesis.

THE SCIENTIFIC (R)EVOLUTION

There are (at least) two ways to tell the story of modern science: revolution and evolution. Some favour revolution: centuries of medieval darkness followed by an unprecedented breakthrough. Suddenly Nicholas Copernicus puts the sun at the centre of the solar system,

---

89   Ed. Jeff Hardin, Ronald L. Numbers, Ronald A. Binzley, *The Warfare between Science and Religion: The Idea That Wouldn't Die* (Johns Hopkins University Press, 2018)

and—"Let there be light!"—science is created. But this creation story has some large holes in it. The evidence seems to point in another direction. Below I will share with you a much more evolutionary model for the development of science. And it begins not in the 16th century, but much earlier. To understand it we will travel back in time to put ourselves into the mindset of an ancient astronomer.

Until the 16th century, the earth was assumed to be at the centre of the universe, with the sun, moon and stars orbiting around it. We might imagine that ancient thinkers were proud of this fact—having the universe revolve around them. But it wasn't a boast. For them, the heavens were where the more perfect beings existed. Earth, being at the bottom, was the sump of the cosmos! Famous teachers of the earth-centred model were the Greek philosopher Aristotle (c. 384–322 BC) and Ptolemy (AD 100–170), an Egyptian astronomer. Ptolemy provided the mathematics to map onto Aristotle's model, and even though his maths was intricate (and at points highly improbable), the main thing was that it worked— at least well enough to predict the movements of the stars and planets. But there were problems.

A central feature of the ancient Greek worldview was the idea of fate and necessity. Aristotle saw all things unfolding by an all-determining reason. Neither the gods nor humanity nor the world were free. Everything was the way it had to be. So, on a question like "What shape are the orbits of the planets?" Aristotle would answer, *Circular, because the circle is the most perfect shape and, in all the cosmos, heavenly bodies are the closest to perfection.*

Notice the assumptions: there is a way things must be that is baked into the fabric of the cosmos. The orbits of the planets are fixed by reason, and we can access that reason by thinking carefully. Investigating the world with our senses is not that reliable—after all, our senses can deceive us. For Aristotle and his followers, studying the world was less a journey "outwards" into the surprising ways things *are*, and more a journey of the mind "upwards" into the predictable ways things *must be*. All this made the Greeks brilliant at reasoning and indifferent to experimentation.

But the Bible presented a very different picture and therefore provided profoundly different foundations for the understanding of the world. Let's explore three features of biblical teaching which are taught in the first three chapters of the Bible: truths about God, the world and humanity.

THE GENESIS OF MODERN SCIENCE
"In the beginning" there was God (Genesis 1:1). This is our origin, according to Genesis. And because God exists before and behind the universe, it means God is unconstrained. Unlike the ancient Greek idea of an eternal universe, the God of the Bible does not have to make do with a pre-existing world, nor must he conform to laws or logic that exists outside him. God is free. When he chooses to make the world, he shapes it by his own creative Voice so that it's exactly as he wants it. "God saw all that he had made, and it was very good" (Genesis 1:31).

The earth has one moon (v 16), but it could have had three or nine. Why one? The answer does not lie in the logical necessity of a single-mooned earth. The deepest answer is simply "Because God..." And if you want to figure out how many moons the earth—or any planet—actually has, you ought to go and check.

This holds true for everything in the natural world. The shape of the planetary orbits might be circular, or God might have chosen to make them triangular for all we know. Nothing can be assumed. Everything must be tested. This is because if God is free, then the universe could be otherwise than it is—it could be any way that God chooses. You might think that the world *must be* a certain way. But there is no must. You need to investigate what actually *is*. The freedom of God became a foundational concept for the way Christians came to approach science.

A second important conviction was that the world can be figured out—and figured out by little old humans. Philosophers of science use more technical terms for this foundation—like "intelligibility" or "comprehensibility"—but what they mean is the figure-out-ability of the universe. There are regularities in the way the world works, and those regularities are reliable—they hold true both now and back in the Jurassic Age; both here and far away on Jupiter. This amounts to a belief that the universe is reliably ordered. But there is another belief involved too: the conviction that humans can understand this order.

It's astonishing that these two truths should hold. Astrophysicist Neil deGrasse Tyson has marvelled that "the goings-on within the three-pound human brain are what enabled us to figure out our place in the universe."[90] Here we find a stunning co-ordination between the universe and the human brain. Our brains are a part of the physical universe (an infinitesimal part in the grand scheme of things) that can, to a degree, understand the whole. Astonishingly, we find the universe figure-out-able. Albert Einstein was so amazed by this fact that he called it a miracle: "The eternal mystery of the world is its comprehensibility ... The fact that it is comprehensible is a miracle."[91]

Such a miracle is the fundamental precondition for science. Yet, why should the world be like this? And why should our minds be in such a privileged position? Those questions are difficult to answer on atheist foundations. If our minds are purely survival machines, that doesn't give us great confidence in their truth-seeking abilities. But if we turn to Genesis 1, we find the kind of world and the kind of human abilities which science requires.

On page one of the Bible we meet an orderly God who has made an orderly world and placed humanity right at the intersection of heaven and earth. Humanity is "in the image of God", and we have "dominion" over the earth (Genesis 1:26-27). If you put aside the Bible, the fact that the mysteries of the cosmos can be probed by a three-pound (1.4kg) human brain is an unexplained miracle. For an atheist, it's a miracle without a miracle-maker. Yet with Genesis 1 in hand, the miracle makes sense, and the foundations of science are laid.

---

90   Neil deGrasse Tyson, "Cosmic Perspective". https://www.naturalhistorymag.com/universe/201367/cosmic-perspective. Accessed 31st October 2021.

91   Albert Einstein, *Out of My Later Years* (Citadel Press, 1956), p 61.

So Genesis 1 teaches the freedom of God and the figure-out-ability of the world, but all this might give us a false impression. We might imagine that humanity is simply God-like in its comprehension of the cosmos.

If we're tempted to think that, then Genesis 3 gives us a sobering dose of reality. The chapter tells of the fall of humanity. Adam and Eve disobey the Voice of God, and the world is unravelled. Such disobedience goes against the very rationality that made the world, and the consequences affect every part of humanity, including our rational faculties. As soon as it happens, Adam and Eve start doing some seriously stupid things: like hiding from God (a ridiculous game); covering their nakedness with fig-leaves (ridiculous clothing); and covering their guilt with excuses (ridiculous self-justification). Yet their behaviour is more than just ridiculous; it's relatable. We all have a complicated relationship with the truth. The poet T.S. Eliot said, "Humankind cannot bear very much reality." We know we ought to be truth-seekers, but so often we hide from uncomfortable realities, and we excuse our mistakes rather than exposing them.

This provides us with our third important conviction. If we want to do science, we must take this human fallibility into account. This is precisely why the modern scientific method takes the shape that it does. Psychologist Steven Pinker explains it well:

> "The signature practices of science, including open debate, peer review, and double-blind methods, are designed to circumvent the sins to which scientists, being human, are vulnerable. As [physicist] Richard

*Feynman put it, the first principle of science is 'that you
must not fool yourself—and you are the easiest person
to fool.'"*[92]

So these are three foundational teachings from Genesis:
the freedom of God; the figure-out-ability of the world;
and the fallibility of humans. Press deeply into these
truths—as Christians did, especially in the Middle
Ages—and what you get is a scientific evolution. Let's
trace the medieval development.

STANDING ON THE SHOULDERS OF GIANTS

Augustine's most famous and most accessible book,
Confessions (c. 400), was an extended prayer to God. Yet
even in the context of prayer, the north-African bishop
could not help but return to a topic that pervades his
other writings: the freedom of God.

*"You [O God] were, and besides you nothing was. From
nothing, then, you created heaven and earth."*[93]

The creation of the universe "out of nothing" was a vital
theme in Augustine's thinking and became foundational
for Christian theology. It was in stark opposition to that
of Aristotle, who taught that the world had always existed.
But if Aristotle was wrong about that, perhaps he was
wrong about other things. It was Christians who were most
comfortable with challenging the classical assumptions.

For instance, in the eastern Byzantine Empire, John

---

92 Steven Pinker, *Enlightenment Now* (Penguin, 2018), p 390.

93 Augustine, *Confessions*, Book XII, Section 7, trans. R.S. Pine-Coffin (Penguin, 1961),
    p 284-85.

Philoponus (c. AD 490–570) questioned another of Aristotle's beliefs: that motion requires immediate and continuous external force. Aristotle thought that objects (like the planets) move only because they are being pushed very directly by a mover. This led him and his contemporaries to think that the stars and planets were being constantly nudged along by spiritual powers, or that perhaps they were spiritual powers, chugging through the heavens.

But the assumptions they were working with were easily disproved if only you ran some experiments. Today a simple game of darts would teach you that objects can move without a mover constantly pushing them (unless your tactic is to refuse to throw the dart and instead to walk up to the board and stick it into the bullseye—but this approach is frowned on). Aristotle thought of the planets as like darts in the hand of that cheating darts player. But John Philoponus knew from experience that objects do not need always to be pushed—sometimes they can be thrown. They can move on the basis of an initial impetus given to them. And if that is so, then perhaps the stars and planets have been set in motion and are wheeling around in the heavens without the need for constant pushing. The problem for Philoponus was figuring out why the stars and planets were not slowing down to a standstill. If they were not being pushed, surely friction would stop them.

Fast-forward to the age of universities and here we meet the "natural philosophers"—scholars reasoning about the natural world. It would be anachronistic to call them scientists, but it's also unlikely that modern science would have developed without them. That was the view of philosopher and mathematician Alfred North Whitehead (1861–1947). He was not a Christian; nevertheless he was certain that science had emerged from within a Christian context because of the widespread "faith in the possibility of science ... derivative from medieval theology".[94]

A core belief for the medievals was in the "two books": the book of God (Scripture) and the book of nature (the universe). This was at the heart of their faith in the figure-out-ability of the world. We can study the Bible to know God, and we can study the world to know his handiwork. Both are important, and both were pursued with rigour and reverence. One such philosopher was William of Ockham (1295–1347). At Oxford University he applied himself to some of Philoponus's questions. William forwarded the idea (not original to him) that space was a frictionless vacuum and that ongoing impetus can be given to an object (a forerunner to Newton's first law of motion).

Next came Nicole d'Oresme (1325–1382) from the University of Paris, who established that the earth turns on its axis. This, though, raised many questions— it certainly doesn't feel like the earth is spinning at a thousand miles an hour! Many brought challenges to the theory. But answering challenges was integral to university life as it developed in the Middle Ages. The fact that faculties were competing for the best scholars meant that robust argumentation was the essence of the intellectual life. "The fallibility of humans" was

---

94   A. N. Whitehead, *Science and the Modern World* (Cambridge University Press, 1926), p 16.

fully appreciated, and debate was encouraged as a countermeasure. Step forward Nicholas of Cusa (1401–1464) from the University of Padua to successfully answer many of the objections to d'Oresme's discovery.

Finally, in the early 16th century, Nicholas Copernicus (1473–1543) from the University of Padua put the sun in the centre and the earth in the heavens: job done! Except that it wasn't.

Copernicus's system was no better than Ptolemy's for predicting astronomical events, and it included almost as much intricacy and improbability. His problem was that, along with Aristotle, he assumed circular orbits. Copernicus then followed Ptolemy's workaround; to make the model work, he had to invent scores of miniature loops in the orbits of the planets (which were not observed). "Consequently, everything in Copernicus's famous book *On the Revolutions of the Heavenly Spheres* is wrong, other than the placement of the sun at the center."[95] In terms of actual observations, the evidence did not favour Copernicus (nor Galileo, who took up the Copernican view). Those sun-centred (heliocentric) astronomers happened to be right, but "the science" was against them.

It took Johannes Kepler (1571–1639) to realise that the orbits were elliptical, and it took Isaac Newton (1642–1727) and his theory of gravity to explain why these heavenly bodies moved the way they did—why, for instance, they orbited rather than lassoed off into space. At *that* point there was a coherent system of astronomy

---

95   Rodney Stark, *The Triumph of Christianity* (Bravo Ltd, 2012), p 280.

and physics that actually agreed with observations and could make improved predictions. But these things did not happen in a single "Eureka" moment. Isaac Newton famously said, "If I have seen further it is by standing on the shoulders of Giants."[96] (Fittingly enough, that phrase was itself an invention of the Middle Ages.)

In the last two chapters we have seen that there was no sudden "Let there be light" after a millennium of darkness. There was no miraculous bloom following the sandy desert of the Middle Ages. The scientific revolution was in fact an evolution. The celebrated historian of science I. Bernard Cohen notes, "The idea that a Copernican revolution in science occurred goes counter to the evidence ... and is the invention of later historians."[97] Just as medieval Christendom gave us human rights, universities, parliaments and more, it also prepared the way for science. The "conflict thesis" regarding faith and science does not stack up when you examine the evidence.

HANG ON: THE CASE OF GALILEO GALILEI

At this stage, proponents of the conflict thesis will want to play their trump card: Galileo.

Born in Pisa and educated at its university, Galileo became the greatest physicist the world had ever seen, the inventor of the finest telescope in history, and, according

---

96   Isaac Newton, "Letter from Sir Isaac Newton to Robert Hooke", Historical Society of Pennsylvania. https://discover.hsp.org/Record/dc-9792/Description#tabnav. Accessed 11th September 2021.

97   Quoted in Rodney Stark, *For The Glory of God* (Princeton University Press, 2003), p 139.

to the Roman Catholic Church, a heretic. If you want to tell a "religion versus science" story, Galileo is the hero for you. He was condemned for the crime of following the science and daring to doubt church dogma. It seems an open-and-shut case, but it's worth ensuring we have our facts in order.

When Galileo championed the Copernican model, both the data and the scientific consensus were against him. This became a problem in 1616 when the church, having consulted with the most prominent astronomers of the day, picked a side. They declared heliocentrism (the sun-centred model) to be heretical. This was, without doubt, a high crime against the kind of free enquiry which drives science. Here is the negative side of the church's involvement in science. For centuries, before and after this incident, the church was the world's greatest patron of astronomy. But 1616 was very much the wrong kind of involvement. And, with the benefit of hindsight, they backed the wrong horse entirely.

Notice, though, that this was not a case of the church backing the Scriptures against the scientists. They backed a majority of scientists against a minority. And as for the Scriptures, they put themselves on record as willing to change their mind with incontrovertible evidence. All sides cited Augustine, who taught a thousand years earlier that biblical interpretation should not and cannot be opposed to assured truths discovered in nature. Yet the church insisted (and most astronomers agreed) that the Copernican view was not at all assured.

So while it might be tempting to cast the Galileo affair

as a debate between the enlightened forces of science and the benighted church powers, historian of science Maurice Finocchiaro observes a more complex picture: "Rather than having an ecclesiastical monolith on one side clashing with a scientific monolith on the other, the real conflict was between two attitudes that criss-crossed both".[98] There were "progressives" and "conservatives" in both the church and the scientific community. Galileo has become a symbol of the brave pioneer standing foursquare behind "the science", but there was no such thing as "the science", and at this stage the evidence and the scientific community were leaning the other way.

When his friend became pope, Galileo saw an opportunity to get his views heard. He asked for permission from Pope Urban VIII to write a book laying out the two views of the solar system side by side. The pope obliged but then sorely regretted it when, in 1632, Galileo published a popular dialogue between the sun-centred and earth-centred views. The earth-centred proponent was named Simplicio. Galileo even put the pope's own words into the mouth of this "Simpleton". In the words of David Bentley Hart, it all descended into an "idiotic ... conflict between men of titanic egotism".[99] To the church's shame, they tried Galileo in 1633, yet the irony was that in this famous "faith versus science" trial, "it was the church that was demanding proof, and Galileo who was demanding blind assent—to a model that was wrong."[100]

---

98 Maurice A. Finocchiaro, *The Warfare Between Science and Religion* (Johns Hopkins University Press, 2018), p 33.

99 David Bentley Hart, *Atheist Delusions* (Yale University Press, 2010), p 65.

100 As above, p 66.

In the end Galileo was found to be "vehemently suspect of heresy", and he lived out the rest of his days under house arrest.

Protestants, like the father of modern chemistry Robert Boyle (1627–1691) and the poet John Milton (1608–1674), were the first to fix upon this incident as the quintessence of Roman Catholic perversity. For them the parallels with the Luther story were too strong to ignore—a pioneering thinker shot down by an ignorant pope. But for those, like David Bentley Hart, who are uninterested in the points-scoring of "Protestant versus Catholic", we shouldn't miss the wood for the trees. To focus on the Galileo affair...

> "... obscure[s] the rather significant reality that, in the sixteenth and seventeenth centuries, Christian scientists educated in Christian universities and following a Christian tradition of scientific and mathematical speculation overturned a pagan cosmology and physics, and arrived at conclusions that would have been unimaginable within the confines of the [ancient Greek] scientific traditions."[101]

Whatever else we learn from the examples of Copernicus, Galileo, Kepler and Newton, it ought to be obvious that modern science was invented nowhere else but among devout Christians in a devoutly Christian age, drawing explicitly on Christian beliefs and practices. Let's listen to their own convictions about faith and science.

---

101 As above, p 65.

THE MIRACLE OF SCIENCE

Copernicus: *"To know the mighty works of God, to comprehend ... the wonderful workings of His laws, surely all this must be a pleasing and acceptable mode of worship to the Most High."*[102]

Galileo: *"The glory and greatness of Almighty God are marvelously discerned in all his works."*[103]

Kepler: *"Geometry is unique and eternal, a reflection of the mind of God. That men are able to participate in it is one of the reasons why man is an image of God."*[104]

Newton: *"This most beautiful system of the sun, planets, and comets could only proceed from the counsel and dominion of an Intelligent Powerful Being."*[105]

Science emerged among people who believed certain things. Specifically, they believed that science could be done. They believed in what Einstein called "the miracle of comprehensibility"—the wonder that puny human brains can figure out the mysteries of the cosmos. They trusted in this miracle because they believed that humans are made in God's image. And what is perhaps more fascinating than these beliefs is the fact that such beliefs

102 Louis E. Van Norman, *Poland: The Knight Among Nations* (Fleming H. Revell, 1907), p 290.

103 *Letter to Madame Christina of Lorraine, Grand Duchess of Tuscany* (1615). https://inters.org/Galilei-Madame-Christina-Lorraine. Accessed 2nd February 2022.

104 Letter (9 or 10 April 1599) to Herwart von Hohenburg, as quoted in "Epilogue", *The Sleepwalkers: A History of Man's Changing Vision of the Universe* (Hutchinson, 1959), p 524.

105 "The General Scholium to Isaac Newton's *Principia mathematica*". https://web.archive.org/web/20100524103006/http://www.isaacnewton.ca/gen_scholium/scholium.htm. Accessed 2nd February 2022.

were rewarded. It turns out that the world is open to this kind of investigation and that human minds are fit for the task. This did not need to be the case. But the world showed itself to be the kind of place that Copernicus and company believed it to be. What's more, humans appeared to be the kinds of creatures these Christians assumed they were. Since Copernicus, we have witnessed five centuries of extraordinary scientific advance built on these assumptions. The foundations appear strong.

A great many scientists today are not Christian, of course. Some are anti-Christian. But all of them must depend on Einstein's miracle. Many will dislike the language of miracle. They may insist that their belief in science is based not on religious reasons but on pragmatic ones: it delivers. They may say that they have evidence: centuries of scientific advance. They trust science because it works. This is all true. Science does work. But we ought to be curious about *why* it works. And with every scientific discovery, we ought to be further convinced of Einstein's miracle (and still more inquisitive about why it should hold). In a sense you could view the whole of science as a giant experiment testing the hypothesis that the world is as "miraculous" as Einstein said. The hypothesis looks more assured with every scientific advance.

THE ADVANCE OF THE LIGHT

Thomas Jefferson painted a compelling picture: "enlightenment versus the priests". We love this kind of conflict story in which the light advances and the religious powers flee, shrieking, into the shadows. The power of the story seems to trump all evidence against it.

It doesn't seem to matter how historically bogus are the claims of its story-tellers; neither does it seem to matter how Christian were the founders of modern science, how theological were their motivations, how apt their worldview proved in the investigation of nature, how invested the church has been in the scientific enterprise or how widespread faith is among contemporary scientists. Ironically none of this evidence seems important. What persists is a compelling story of light versus darkness / science versus religion. The idea will not die. Why?

Perhaps the reason we love this story is because it's a version of the great story—the one that built our world. Christ came calling himself the light. He was the light leading us out of darkness (John 8:12), and he was the truth who would set us free (John 8:32). But he was opposed by the priests. The Jewish leaders of his day handed him over to death, and on the cross the light was extinguished and the truth was silenced—such is the inclination of religious powers. Nevertheless, the Light was victorious, the Truth rose again, and liberation and new life were unleashed on the world. This is the ultimate narrative that other lesser stories have echoed: Martin Luther shining spiritual light into the priestly darkness; Galileo declaring truth to a simpleton pope.

By the time the story was retold by Jefferson, it had undergone several rewrites. Now Christianity, in its totality, was the arch-opponent of science, twisting its handlebar moustache while science rode in on a white horse to save the day. These are powerful stereotypes, and they exert a significant grip on our Christian-shaped imaginations, but fitting the record of history to this story proves the difficult part. Ironically, to make science the unquestioned and unaided hero of the piece requires so many fudges, fibs and flips that its proponents end up denying the evidence. The conflict story turns out to be a religious myth, and when we examine the data, we cannot help but notice that science emerged in a Christian context for Christian reasons. Today, as science continues to advance, these convictions are not being vanquished; they are being vindicated. The light of science is not driving out Christianity—the very opposite. Christian convictions (whether acknowledged or not) have been holding the torch from the beginning.

7. FREEDOM

"You can't, in 21st-century Britain, have a slaver on a statue."

— Sir Keir Starmer, 2020

The leader of the UK's Labour party spoke for many. It was June 2020 and, following George Floyd's death, anti-racism protests had erupted all over the world. In Bristol, protestors toppled the statue of Edward Colston, which had stood in the city for 125 years. Keir Starmer wished it had come down via the democratic process, but come down it must. It's 21st-century Britain.

Colston in his day (1636–1721) was a successful merchant, a generous philanthropist, a professing Christian and a member of the Royal Africa Company, which traded West African slaves to the Americas for obscene profits. It has been estimated that during his twelve years with the company, 84,000 African men, women and children were captured and shipped across the Atlantic to be worked to death on tobacco and sugar plantations.

This was part of the Atlantic slave trade (16th to 19th centuries), when more than 12 million Africans were captured, bought, sold, trafficked and exploited ruthlessly by mainly white, mainly Christian owners. In 21st-century Britain—and especially in June 2020— nothing and no one associated with this evil would be able to stand.

But it did stand. Or rather, British society stood upon the practice and had done so for hundreds of years. Human trafficking propped up so much of the British Empire's expansion and wealth. In a cruel irony, it even funded great works of philanthropy. In 1721 Colston died as "the great benefactor of the city of Bristol", having donated the equivalent of £5.5 million to charity.[106] In his day he was considered a good man—even a great man. 299 years later they had to fetch his statue from the harbour, and his charitable trusts have either changed their name or disbanded completely. In the space of three centuries, we have gone from revering to reviling a man like Edward Colston. This chapter explores how it happened, and why.

A SECULAR CREED

"We hold these truths to be self-evident, that all men are created equal, that they are endowed by their Creator with certain unalienable Rights, that among these are Life, Liberty and the pursuit of Happiness."
(*Declaration of Independence, 1776*)

These words have functioned like a secular creed for the American Republic.[107] Over the centuries US leaders have held themselves and their people to these "self-evident" truths. Thomas Jefferson, the chief author of the declaration, might be familiar to you from the last chapter. He was the man who considered priests to be fleeing the

---

106   David Hughson, *London* (J. Stratford, 1808), p 386.

107   For more on the ways our modern values represent a "secular creed", I recommend Rebecca McLaughlin's book of the same name, *The Secular Creed* (The Gospel Coalition, 2021).

advance of science like witches flee the approach of day. He went on to become the third president of the United States and the owner of 600 slaves. All of which alerts us to the fact that truths espoused (whether in secular or religious creeds) are not always truths owned and applied. Nevertheless, the words of such creeds can perform much better than their authors.

In 1858, Abraham Lincoln cited the declaration's "majestic interpretation of the economy of the Universe" and made the application directly to the issue of slavery: "Nothing stamped with the Divine image and likeness was sent into the world to be trodden on, and degraded, and imbruted by its fellows".[108] A century later, Martin Luther King Jr. called this sentence from the declaration "a promissory note" to America's citizens—a promissory note which America had defaulted on. So then, at its founding (18th century), through its defining struggle with slavery (19th century), and then in the civil-rights movement (20th century), America's leaders have returned to these words as though they were Holy Writ. Indeed, in their speeches Lincoln and King would weave together the declaration and Scripture because, in truth, without biblical foundations Jefferson's words are faintly absurd.

To imagine that human rights and equality are "self-evident" is audacious to say the least. Self-evident truths are things like "all triangles have three sides" and "all bachelors are unmarried". They should be things you can't not know. But outside of a biblical foundation, no

108 "Speech at Lewistown, Illinois", 17th August 1858. https://quod.lib.umich.edu/l/lincoln/lincoln2/1:567?rgn=div1;view=fulltext. Accessed 19th November 2021.

one in history—including the world's greatest thinkers and moralists—has known about human rights. No one has seen in humans an inherent dignity and value *simply by virtue of their membership of the human race.* A survey of human civilisations reveals that the only thing self-evident about human rights is that they are not self-evident.

If we're looking for a human universal, slavery is a much stronger candidate: "All known societies above the very primitive level have been slave societies".[109] Slavery is a universal. Rights? Rights are weird—"nonsense on stilts" as the philosopher Jeremy Bentham (1748–1832) characterised them.[110]

So how have we come to believe in these magical properties—and to believe in them as though they are a self-evident, natural endowment? To quote Yuval Noah Harari again:

> *"The Americans got the idea of equality from Christianity, which argues that every person has a divinely created soul, and that all souls are equal before God. However, if we do not believe in the Christian myths about God, creation and souls, what does it mean that all people are 'equal'?"*[111]

Without that specific Christian inheritance, it means little.

---

109   Rodney Stark, *The Triumph of Christianity* (Bravo Ltd, 2012), p 376.

110   "Natural rights is simple nonsense: natural and imprescriptible rights, rhetorical nonsense—nonsense upon stilts" (Jeremy Bentham, *A Critical Examination of the Declaration of Rights*, 1843)

111   Yuval Noah Harari, *Sapiens: A Brief History of Humankind* (Vintage, 2015), p 109.

How then can we take the Declaration of Independence seriously? It seems that this key sentence from the declaration can only be said with integrity if all the emphasis is put on the first word. *"We* hold these truths to be self-evident." It's a case of *"We* choose to stand on this unique foundation. Billions wouldn't. But *we* do. This, *for us,* will be the moral equivalent of 'triangles have three sides'."

All of this is perfectly possible as a faith position (it has served the United States well for nearly a quarter of a millennium), but at times the foundations need to be examined. When we do that, we recognise what Tom Holland has pointed out:

> "That all men had been created equal, and endowed
> with an inalienable right to life, liberty and the
> pursuit of happiness, were not remotely self-evident
> truths. That most Americans believed they were owed
> less to philosophy than to the Bible: to the assurance
> given equally to Christians and Jews, to Protestants
> and Catholics, to Calvinists and Quakers, that every
> human being was created in God's image. The truest
> and ultimate seedbed of the American republic—no
> matter what some of those who had composed its
> founding documents might have cared to think—was
> the book of Genesis."[112]

The Enlightenment values of the declaration can be taken seriously when we recognise that those "Enlightenment values" are biblical. Without a grounding in the Scriptures,

---

112   Tom Holland, *Dominion* (Little, Brown, 2019), p 400.

such convictions are a castle in the air. To be fair, the castle is very large. There are now billions of residents, and they include people of all faiths and none. (It's actually rare nowadays to meet someone who disbelieves in human rights and equality. When we find such a specimen, we're pretty quick to ban them from Facebook.)

But then how is this castle still standing? How have so many people come to believe in essentially biblical values while comparatively few recognise the source? It's not because these values are self-evident (they are anything but); it's because they have become evident in certain historical developments. It's a little like what happened with the scientific (r)evolution. As we saw last chapter, modern science grew out of distinctively Christian soil, but its spectacular fruits have been enjoyed by all. On a moral level, the abolition of the slave trade has had a very similar effect. It has also grown out of Christian convictions which we now take to be universal. But it's worth examining the roots.

In the 18th and 19th centuries Christians, acting for distinctively Christian reasons, did something no one had ever done. They drove the abolition of the slave trade, overturning a practice present in all times and places in history. To say as much is not just the enthusiasm of Christian partisans. The pre-eminent historian of transatlantic slavery, David Brion Davis has written that "religion was the central concern of all the British abolitionist leaders", without which "the fall of New World slavery could not have occurred", and that this amounts to "a moral achievement that may have no parallel."[113]

Abolition was not an Enlightenment movement. As the former archbishop of Canterbury, Rowan Williams, has said, "If the abolition of slavery had been left to enlightened secularists in the eighteenth century, we would still be waiting."[114] But the success of this Christian movement has been so complete that we share its outlook as though it were obvious. We're all born free now. The hard-won political, legal, and—in the case of the US Civil War—military battles mean that *of course* we consider freedom our birthright. Yesterday's victory has become today's commonplace. And now we look back at former times bewildered that life could ever have been otherwise.

We are like children looking back at their parents' photo album and wondering, "How could those hairstyles have ever been in fashion?" More searchingly, we ask, "How could those beliefs have ever been accepted?" As children of the Christian revolution, we have serious questions for our parents: "How could you ever have allowed things to get like that?" This is the subject of our next "Hang On".

HANG ON: ISN'T CHRISTIANITY PRO-SLAVERY?

When we consider Christianity and slavery, we might picture the deeply religious Edward Colston or a southern United States slaveholder who justified their evil with

---

113   D.B. Davis, *Slavery and Human Progress* (Oxford University Press, 1986), p 139; *Inhuman Bondage: The Rise and Fall of New World Slavery* (Oxford University Press, 2006), p 331.

114   Quoted in John Dickson, *Bullies and Saints* (Zondervan, 2021), p 111.

Scriptures at the ready. On the other hand, we might think of William Wilberforce (1759–1833), an evangelical Christian Member of Parliament who made abolition his life's work. But perhaps what we need more than either is to picture someone like Frederick Douglass (1817–1895).

Born in Maryland in the US, Douglass was enslaved for the first 20 years of his life and beaten continually by supposedly Christian slave owners. When he escaped, he became a famous abolitionist, a friend of Abraham Lincoln, and an internationally renowned speaker, writer and *preacher*. Indeed, it was his Christian faith that most powerfully informed his abolitionism. Hear him rail against the institution with Genesis in hand:

> *"There can no more be a law for the enslavement of man, made in the image of God, than for the enslavement of God himself."*[115]

Here is the power of the preacher. Whereas Thomas Jefferson could convict you of violating self-evident truth, Frederick Douglass makes the bondsman an enslaver of God. This openly religious language was the style of abolitionism that carried the day. But notice the preacher himself: like millions of others, he was a former slave who adopted the religion of his master, not as a forced conversion but as a kind of subversive liberation. Religious revivals occurred, first in the West Indies (in the 18th century) and then in America (around the turn of the 19th century). The preachers carrying the

---

115 Frederick Douglass, *Selected Speeches and Writings* (Chicago Review Press, 2000), p 161.

message were sometimes missionaries from overseas and sometimes former slaves themselves. The "Negro spirituals" they sang embodied the Christianity that was so resonant: one that identified with Moses in Egypt, with Israel in bondage and with the great Sufferer, Christ: "Nobody knows the trouble I've seen, nobody knows but Jesus". Their songs gave full voice to lament but also dared to hope for a promised land, looking forward to the day when heaven's "sweet chariot [was] comin' for to carry me home."

The message was one of redemption and the effect was remarkable. Howard Thurman (1899–1981), a great influence on Martin Luther King, wrote, "By some amazing but vastly creative spiritual insight, the slave undertook the redemption of the religion that the master had profaned in his midst."[116] Those who were despised and degraded found in Christ a dignity and hope denied them by their "Christian" enslavers.

"If slavery is the founding sin of America," writes Rebecca McLaughlin, "the existence of the black church is perhaps its greatest miracle".[117] But it's a miracle close to the heart of Christian faith. As Mary, the mother of Jesus, sang in Luke chapter 1:

"[The Lord] has brought down rulers from their thrones
but has lifted up the humble.
He has filled the hungry with good things

---

116 Quoted in James H. Cone, *The Cross and the Lynching Tree* (Orbis, 2011), p 133-134.

117 Rebecca McLaughlin, *Confronting Christianity: 12 Hard Questions for the World's Largest Religion* (Crossway, 2019) p 190.

but has sent the rich away empty.
He has helped his servant Israel,
  remembering to be merciful." (Luke 1:52-54)

When enslaved believers turned to the Old Testament, they did not find, as their owners claimed to, a justification for their enslavement. (Both Testaments condemn "man-stealing"; if followed, this would have cut the throat of both Roman and Atlantic slavery—Exodus 21:16; 1 Timothy 1:10.) Instead, they discovered an experience like their own: a people held captive in Egypt yet favoured by God, who takes their side against their oppressors, judges their captors and brings them out to a land flowing with milk and honey. This was the defining event for the Old Testament and the pattern of Christ's New Testament redemption.

The grand sweep of the Bible narrates the story of "servant Israel" being freed. There is bondage and then liberation. That is the big picture. The details are also important, although some of them are difficult, especially for modern readers. In the Old Testament Law of Moses there was a practice of slavery. It was different to anything practised in Rome or the Americas, but still, it does not read at all like the UN Declaration of Human Rights. One key to understanding it—the key to understanding the whole of the Old Testament—is to fit it into the bigger narrative.

Within the Old Testament there was a once-in-a-generation celebration called Jubilee—a time when all Israelite slaves were released and all debts were cancelled. Debt and slavery went together in Israelite thinking because, at its heart, their brand of slavery was a temporary solution to bankruptcy. But beyond the Old Testament we see how the Jubilee was fulfilled.

When Jesus preached his first sermon (Luke 4:16-21) he declared himself to be the long-promised Liberator. Specifically, he declared a once-and-for-all Jubilee: "[The Lord] has sent me ... to set the oppressed free, to proclaim the year of the Lord's favour" (Luke 4:18-19). But to bring such liberation required Jesus to give up his life. He embraced the slave's death so that those who are slaves of sin—which is to say, all of us—might live his life of freedom. The shadow of the old was swallowed up in the light of Christ's victory. The bonds of sin and death were broken at Easter and a "promised land" of freedom beckoned.

Where did that leave the Old Testament practice? Remember the way that Jesus handled the question of marriage and divorce in Matthew 19? In that instance he spoke of Moses' legislation as a non-ideal response to the Israelites' "hardness of heart". But Christ had come to restore things to the pattern laid out in Genesis 1 and 2—his purposes for us are not slavery but dominion.

This is how the New Testament and the early church saw slavery. In Christ, slavery was abolished, even if in the Roman empire it was rampant. In the church there were only brothers and sisters before the Lord. In society the evil remained, and Christians considered it, like poverty, as a dark and stubborn feature of this fallen world—something which churches and individuals could work towards improving, perhaps by purchasing the freedom of slaves (which they did, sometimes redeeming thousands at a time). But precious few could envision this world without it.

In 379, the bishop Gregory of Nyssa went one step further: he condemned the institution of slavery wholesale and demanded its abolition. Yet the fact that Gregory was an outlier even among Christians goes to show the deep roots that slavery had in the ancient imagination. We might wish that the New Testament contained chapters like Gregory's tirade or that the upshot of his righteous indignation was a political movement for change. But whether the issue was infanticide or blood sports or slavery, the New Testament pursued a different kind of reform. Jesus said his kingdom would grow like a tiny seed becoming the largest plant, or like yeast working its way through the whole batch of dough (Matthew 13:31-33). We desire an abrupt reckoning; Jesus speaks of slow but inexorable growth. To be honest, the former makes a much better biopic, and so generally we are impatient with quietism. But even before the moral campaigning of the 18th century, the "slow and steady" approach had made great gains.

After Rome fell in 410, slavery in those western territories began dissolving away. Soon after the 9th century slavery had all but vanished from northern Europe. By the 11th century it had virtually gone from central Italy and France. By 1200 it had largely disappeared in England.[118] Here is yet another surprising development during the Middle Ages.

---

118   Hugh Thomas, *The Slave Trade* (Simon and Schuster, 2013), p 794.

Many factors were involved in these changes, including economic and technological improvements, as well as the devastating effects of plagues, which smashed through society at every level. But part of it too was spiritual beliefs and legislation working in tandem. Baptism (the ritual washing which marks membership of the church) and the Lord's Supper (the commemorative meal of bread and wine) were offered to everyone in the church of Christ, slaves included. Therefore, it became impossible, theologically, to deny the full personhood of those who were members of the same spiritual community. Laws began to be enacted which forbade the enslavement of fellow "brothers and sisters", and increasingly the equality of the spiritual community began to be reflected in the political realm too. Before we ever got to the Renaissance, slavery had melted away in much of Europe: another bright development in that "dark" medieval age.

After 1492, though, the evil erupted again with the conquest of the Americas, first by the Spanish Empire, with the Portuguese, Dutch and British to follow. They all proved as cruel and domineering as any empires in history, with one difference: the name in which they conquered. Atrocities have been committed in the name of every god and every ideology, including Christ's. But such evils done in the name of Jesus appear especially jarring. Tom Holland notes the problem for *Christian* imperialists:

> *"No people in antiquity would ever have succeeded in winning an empire for themselves had they doubted their licence to slaughter and enslave the vanquished;*

but Christians could not so readily be innocent in their cruelty. When scholars in Europe sought to justify the Spanish conquest of the New World, they reached not for the Church Fathers, but for Aristotle. 'As the Philosopher [Aristotle] says, it is clear that some men are slaves by nature and others free by nature.'"[119]

In his 900-page work, *The Slave Trade*, Hugh Thomas articulates the thinking of the conquistadors: "If Athens had slaves with which to build the Parthenon, and Rome to maintain the aqueducts, why should modern Europe hesitate to have slaves to build its new world in America?" Why indeed? Except for the Christianity which they claimed to honour.

Here we find ourselves circling back to the same issue we've encountered before. As with church abuse, the Crusades, the Spanish Inquisition, and the Galileo affair, the point is not that these things weren't so bad, all things considered. On the contrary, when all things are considered, these events are *truly* evil—Evil with a capital E. But their evil is judged by the good which they pretended to value.

This is why the former slave Frederick Douglass reserved his most scathing criticisms for his fellow "Christians"—and the churches and theologians that sided with slavery. He called them the "bulwark of American slavery". And when he wrote to his old master Thomas Auld in 1848, he pulled no punches, calling the devout churchgoer an "agent of hell".

---

119   Tom Holland, *Dominion* (Little, Brown, 2019), p 307-308.

"The grim horrors of slavery rise in all their ghastly terror before me, the wails of millions pierce my heart, and chill my blood. I remember the chain, the gag, the bloody whip, the deathlike gloom overshadowing the broken spirit of the fettered bondman, the appalling liability of his being torn away from wife and children, and sold like a beast in the market ... It is an outrage upon the soul—a war upon the immortal spirit, and one for which you must give account at the bar of our common Father and Creator."[120]

Notice the "common Father" here. Douglass is able to call his former enslaver both an "agent of hell" and a brother. This is a sophisticated view of both humanity and evil—a view born of the Christianity which both Douglass and Auld professed, but which in actuality confronted them so differently. When the truth of Christ is brought to bear (rather than borrowed as a bulwark for evil), the powerful are brought down and the humble lifted up.

This had always been the spiritual message proclaimed from the Scriptures. But in the 19th century—through decades of campaigning and, in America, a brutal civil war—the spiritual would become manifest in the political. The "self-evident" truth of human equality, which was nothing of the kind, would become evident nonetheless. Slavery, a human universal, would be abolished in the West, and a decidedly Christian conscience would prevail over a bloodstained empire.

---

120 Frederick Douglass, "Letter To Thomas Auld" in *Frederick Douglass: Selected Speeches and Writings* (Lawrence Hill Books, 1999), p 111

PREACHING AND POLITICS

In 1787, the British Abolition Committee was established, made up of Quakers (a countercultural Christian denomination) and evangelicals (biblically-minded Christians in the tradition of the Protestant Reformation). It also included one Member of Parliament: William Wilberforce. Their logo, later made into the hugely popular Wedgwood anti-slavery medallion, depicted a manacled slave on his knees. The caption pricked the conscience of a generation: "Am I not a man and a brother?" Here was Genesis at work again, now viewed through the prism of New Testament Christianity, in which male and female, Jew and Greek, slave and free are all "brothers" in Christ. After the most vigorous moral campaigning Britain had ever seen—including unprecedentedly large petitions, rallies, boycotts, pamphlets, sermons and speeches— the abolition of the trade came in 1807 followed by the emancipation of the slaves in 1833.

Success was achieved in two ways: through preaching and through politics. First, there was an unashamedly Christian message, which moved a generation. In the words of historian Alec Ryrie, "Britain banned a huge, lucrative trade that was one of the principal props of its own empire", and it did so because of abolitionism: "a religious movement first and last".[121]

Preaching was a vital component, but beyond the spiritual authority which abolitionists conveyed, there needed to be political authority to enforce abolition. It certainly helped that Britain "ruled the waves". As the

---

121   Alec Ryrie, *Protestants* (Penguin, 2017), p 196.

world's greatest naval power it could police the Atlantic, and as the world's greatest empire it had the clout to negotiate the spread of abolition and emancipation to other nations.

It was here, in this political phase, that the unashamedly *Christian* distinctives of the abolitionists began to be muted. For abolition to spread from Protestant Britain to Catholic and Muslim lands, there needed to be a work of "translation". Diplomacy required that the language be altered. In 1842 a new phrase was coined. Slavery, said the lawyers, was a crime, not against the Creator, not against Christ, but "a crime against humanity".

> *"The term was one calculated to be acceptable to lawyers of all Christian denominations—and none. Slavery, which only decades previously had been taken almost universally for granted, was now redefined as evidence of savagery and backwardness. To oppose it was to side with progress: To support it was to stand condemned before the bar, not just of Christianity, but of every religion. All of which was liable to come as news to Muslims. In 1842, when the British consul-general to Morocco sought to press the cause of abolitionism, his request that the trade in African slaves be banned was greeted with blank incomprehension. It was a matter, the sultan declared, 'on which all sects and nations have agreed from the time of Adam'."*[122]

The sultan was absolutely right about history. Yet within a generation, he and everyone else found themselves

---

122   Tom Holland, *Dominion* (Little, Brown, 2019), p 430-431.

"on the wrong side" of it. Now we live on this side of abolition, and our moral imaginations find it nearly impossible to leap backwards. The "new normal" is nothing like the old. But with abolition, history seemed to turn a momentous corner and everyone, Christian or not, has been swept up in it. We don't just believe in freedom. Now we believe in progress.

8. PROGRESS

*"The arc of the moral universe is long,
but it bends towards justice."*

— Theodore Parker, 1853

This saying from the anti-slavery campaigner Reverend Theodore Parker (1810–1860) was a favourite of another preacher: Reverend Martin Luther King Jr (1929–1968). In their respective struggles, for the abolition of the slave trade (19th century) and for civil rights (20th century), these men faced grotesque injustice with profound hope. Both men stood in a faith tradition that told them, "Tomorrow could be better than yesterday, though not without immense cost today". The ultimate (but mixed) success of both their struggles has given hope to millions around the world. It has made us all believe that perhaps the universe is moral, and perhaps it is progressing.

Belief in the arc is everywhere: it's in Keir Starmer's belief that Edward Colston's statue cannot stand "in 21st-century Britain". It's in every social commentator's despair that "we are still having this conversation in [insert current year here]". It's in the accusation that a viewpoint is "on the wrong side of history". Apparently, history is headed somewhere—somewhere that can be known in advance. Somewhere better.

Such a belief in progress is not a human universal by any stretch. In previous cultures, it was the past that was viewed as better than the present. After all, the past was really when the heroes and gods were active. Things have been much quieter since. The Greek poet Hesiod (c. 700 BC) came up with five periods of human history, descending from Golden Age to Iron Age. The only way was down (though perhaps we'd cycle back around to experience the whole unravelling again, and again). It was the Bible which proclaimed a unique view of history: not a cycle but an arrow pointing onwards and upwards. The Israelites had come from slavery, yes, but they were heading to "the promised land". The Messiah would come as a Prince of Peace. Though he would suffer, he would nevertheless set the world to rights.

The Old Testament prophets were full of such expectations: after a time of deep shadow, a light would dawn; the valleys would be raised up and the mountains brought low; swords would be beaten into ploughshares (instruments of death becoming instruments of life); Jubilee would be declared (the time when debts are cancelled and slaves released); and in the end, "justice [would] roll on like a river, righteousness like a never-failing stream" (Amos 5:24).

If these phrases sound familiar, you may have heard some of them first from Martin Luther King, perhaps in his spine-tingling "I have a dream" speech. Watch it now online if you want to hear the Hebrew prophets brought to bear on the modern world. Those 17 minutes represent the most powerful case for progress ever made, and they contain more Scripture than many a church sermon.

In fact, King's whole outlook and approach would be unintelligible without his Christian framework.

But while King's belief in the arc of history is profoundly and particularly Christian, it is now shared by millions, of all faiths and none. This has been, in no small part, due to the success of the civil-rights movement. The moral view of history has in turn shaped history, providing yet more evidence for the belief. Now it's a commonplace. Barack Obama had the "moral arc" quotation woven into a rug and placed in the Oval Office.

Steven Pinker, a professor of psychology at Harvard, is so captivated by these ideas that he returns to them repeatedly in his 2018 book, *Enlightenment Now*.[123] In praise of progress, Pinker published 75 graphs regarding such measures as life expectancy, infant mortality, health, wealth, peace, rights, education and much more. All the arrows are going in the right direction. Yet in describing these phenomena, Pinker, an atheist and humanist, cannot help but reach for biblical phrases.

When enthusing about our ability to create clean energy from dismantled nuclear weapons, Pinker calls it "the ultimate beating of swords into plowshares".[124]

When discussing reductions in capital punishment across the world, he confesses that "it makes it seem as if there really is a mysterious arc bending toward justice". Immediately he steps back from the "mysterious" to

---

123 Steven Pinker, *Enlightenment Now: The Case for Reason, Science, Humanism and Progress* (Penguin, 2018).

124 As above, p 149.

explain the trend, adding, "More prosaically, we are seeing a moral principle—Life is sacred, so killing is onerous—become distributed across a wide range of actors and institutions."[125] It's not mysterious, says Pinker. It's just that *the sanctity of life*—a concept unknown to the classical world—is somehow working its way into various aspects of world affairs.

When discussing equality, Pinker wants to "plumb the depths of the current that carries equal rights along". He phrases his question with a deliberate biblical allusion: "Does justice roll on like a river, righteousness like a mighty stream?"[126] The rest of his chapter answers with an emphatic "Yes".

When exploring "the worldwide progress against racism, sexism, and homophobia", Pinker gets the distinct impression that there is an "overarching sweep". He cites again the idea of the "moral arc", promising that while Theodore Parker "could not complete the arc by sight but [only] 'divine it by conscience'", Pinker can offer "a more objective way of determining whether there is a historical arc towards justice".[127] He wants us to know that history's moral progress is not simply an article of faith; it is demonstrable by the data. But whether it's soaring oratory or six dozen graphs that convince you, Pinker, Parker and King seem to have one point of agreement: the arc exists. Progress is real.

---

125 As above, p 213.

126 As above, p 215.

127 As above, p 223.

But as we explore the theme of progress, several ear-splitting klaxons should be sounding. There are huge dangers with the idea of progress.

PROBLEMS WITH PROGRESS

In the 19th century, the idea of "progress" was all the rage. The Industrial Revolution was taking root, bringing unprecedented transformations. This is when so many of Pinker's graphs start bending upwards like a hockey stick. The great thinkers of the age were swept up in the optimism. There was Charles Darwin proclaiming biological progress; Georg Hegel proclaiming historical progress; Sigmund Freud proclaiming psychological progress; and Karl Marx proclaiming economic and political progress. These were just a few of the movers and shakers who believed in moving and shaking.

Yet not all their ideas were new. To pick on Marx as an example, it's worth noting how strongly the other values we have explored in the previous six chapters resonated with him: especially equality, compassion, enlightenment, and science. His communism, while implacably opposed to the church, was unthinkable without it. In some senses it was an attempt to make the state into the church—a place where, as was said of the early Christian community, "no one claimed that any of their possessions was their own, but they shared everything they had" (Acts 4:32).

"From each according to their ability, to each according to their need," runs the Marxist slogan. No wonder it gained some traction in a Christianised society. The Scriptures taught that God lifts up the lowly while bringing down princes from their thrones. But that is the difference between communism and Christianity: in the Bible, God is the equaliser. If humans take that role into their own hands, bloody revolution is usually the result. The death toll of the 20th century has borne that out. The problem with "power to the people" is... people.

This is the difficulty for all believers in progress who are not believers in the God of justice and mercy above. Whether left wing or right wing, whether communist or fascist, if we are only working on the horizontal plane, then "belief in progress" can become a license to make history in whatever way we choose. Without a pole star above us, we can take matters into our own hands, forging our own path and calling it "historical inevitability". This is one of many reasons why the century of progress was followed by an unparalleled century of violence.

The atrocities of the 20th century leave us with a lump in our throat so large that it chokes all our praises of "human progress". 20 million died in "the Great War" (1914–1918). 75 million died in its sequel (1939–1945). We've mentioned the millions dying for Lenin's Marxist revolution in Russia. Stalin killed tens of millions more. During the three years of his great purge (1934–1936), the Russian dictator executed as many people each week as the Spanish Inquisition killed in three and a half centuries. (That's 750,000 executions in 3 years versus the Inquisition's 5,000 in 350 years). In China between 1958 and 1962, "at least 45 million people were worked, starved or beaten to death".[128] The fact that Chairman

---

128   Frank Dikotter, *Mao's Great Famine* (Bloomsbury, 2010). Synopsis: http://www.frankdikotter.com/books/maos-great-famine/. Accessed 31st October 2021.

Mao called this the "Great Leap Forward" should make us forever dubious about claims to progress.

After the "murder century" many have been anxious to find again a pole star—some fixed point of moral sanity and certainty. When we look back at the evils of the 20th century, though, we are given something quite different. We discover a certainty of sorts, but it isn't so much a star to guide us as a pit to avoid. The pit is called Auschwitz.

NAZI JESUS?

What do we consider "the heaviest blow that ever struck humanity"? Reflecting on the 20th century, we might answer, "Adolf Hitler". Hitler himself answered, "The coming of Christianity". He went on: "This filthy reptile [Christianity] raises its head whenever there is a sign of weakness in the State, and therefore it must be stamped on. We have no sort of use for a fairy story invented by the Jews."[129]

Hitler considered Christianity, in particular the Jew Paul, to have introduced to the world "the deliberate lie". This lie concerns the values of equality and compassion that we have explored in this book. Hitler, to the contrary, believed, "All of nature is a violent struggle between strength and weakness, an eternal victory of the strong over the weak".[130] Incredibly, this was his Christmas message in a piece of propaganda called "The German War Christmas". In reality, such views represent a war

---

129 *Hitler's Table Talk 1941-1944*, ed. Gerhard L. Weinberg and H.R. Trevor-Roper (Enigma Books, 2007), p 472-473.

130 Quoted in Richard Weikart, *Hitler's Religion* (Regnery History, 2016), p 131.

on Christmas—a holiday which celebrates the Jewish Messiah born in weakness and poverty.

Twenty years earlier, when a young Hitler was currying favour with an audience that largely self-identified as Christian, he would speak of himself as a Christian. Yet the "Christianity" he owned even at that stage was the very reverse of the story told for two millennia:

> *"My feeling as a Christian points me to my Lord and Savior as a fighter. It points me to the man who once in loneliness, surrounded only by a few followers, recognized these Jews for what they were and summoned men to fight against them and who, God's truth! was greatest not as a sufferer but as a fighter.*

> *"In boundless love as a Christian and as a man I read through the passage which tells us how the Lord at last rose in His might and seized the scourge [the whip] to drive out of the Temple the brood of vipers and adders. How terrific was his fight against the Jewish poison."*[131]

The absurdity of "Nazi Jesus" would be laughable if it weren't also so hate-filled, if we didn't know where it all led, and if it weren't for the ways that many German Christians themselves would follow suit, proclaiming a nazified Christianity.

In the year Hitler came to power, the chairman of the German Christians (a Protestant movement loyal to the Nazis), set out a vision for the church in Germany. What

---

131   Speech delivered at Munich 12 April 1922; from *The Speeches of Adolf Hitler: April 1922-August 1939. 1,* ed. Norman H. Baynes (Oxford University Press, 1942), p 19-20.

Christians needed, they reckoned, was "liberation from the Old Testament with its Jewish recompense ethic". And while they were at it, "the whole scape-goat and inferiority-type theology of the Rabbi Paul should be renounced".[132] In other words, the first move in nazifying Christianity involved tearing up the Old Testament (three quarters of the Bible), followed by half of the New Testament (the letters of Paul). That left them, essentially, with the biographies of one "Jesus the Messiah the son of David, the son of Abraham" (Matthew 1:1). Which goes to show the impossibility of the task. But that didn't stop them trying.

In 1939 the Reich bishop preached on the heartbeat of Christian ethics: love. But he assured his hearers that *real* Christian love "has a hard, warrior-like face. It hates everything soft and weak because it knows that all life can only then remain healthy and fit for life when everything antagonistic to life, the rotten and the indecent, is cleared out of the way and destroyed."[133] In 1942 (incidentally, the year we now know to be the deadliest of the Holocaust, when 2 million died in Auschwitz alone), the German Christians movement declared, "We are not unacquainted with Christian love and the obligation to the helpless, but we demand that the nation be protected from the feckless and the inferior."[134] Nietzsche would have been proud.

---

132 Alec Ryrie, *Protestants* (Penguin, 2017), p 275.

133 Quoted in Doris Bergen, *Twisted Cross* (University of North Carolina Press, 1996), p 205.

134 Quoted in ed. Peter Matheson, *The Third Reich and the Christian Churches* (T. & T. Clark, 1981), p 6.

But they weren't just drawing on a German philosophical heritage. Shamefully there has been horrendous antisemitism in the church's history. From the earliest times there have been Christians who have accused Jewish people of being "Christ-killers"—never mind the fact that Jesus himself was Jewish and that the ones who executed him were Roman. In medieval Christendom it was even alleged that Jews liked to drink the blood of Christian children (the so-called "blood libel"). If a child went missing or died, this became a pretext for frightening retributions, murders and, in the case of medieval Britain, the expulsion of Jews between 1290 and 1657.

Highly relevant to Nazi antisemitism though was Martin Luther, the leading voice of the Protestant Reformation 400 years earlier and a German hero. At the end of his life he wrote a despicable pamphlet, *The Jews and Their Lies*. Historian Alec Ryrie notes that "the best that can be said of [it] is that it does not openly call for genocide".[135] All of which is to say, once again, that Christians are not the heroes of this history. They are often among the chief perpetrators of evil. This story is not about the virtue of Christians; it is about Jesus, the Jewish Messiah, who judges wickedness—including the wickedness of antisemitism—as the vicious evil it is.

On the other hand, we could tell the tale of Christians in Germany whose faith led them to shield the Jews. We could speak of brave resisters of the Nazi evil. Such people existed. But the point is not so much that there

---

135   Alec Ryrie, *Protestants* (Penguin, 2017), p 266.

were Christians who opposed Naziism—some did; millions didn't. The point is not for us to feel superior to that silent majority—truthfully, if we had lived through the Third Reich, the likelihood of our own heroic resistance would have been painfully slight. The point is that those wanting to align with Naziism had to oppose Christianity—even if they did it while wearing a bishop's mitre. "Nazi Jesus" is not a thing. "Nazi Jesus" simply is not Jesus. Adolf Hitler had turned Christianity on its head. In 2,000 years, no one had managed to invert the message of Jesus as Hitler had. He was, very literally, anti-Christ.

So what do you call the fight to stop him? In the Western imagination, what else could World War II be but a legendary battle against evil?

"HUMANITY" TO THE RESCUE
In 1941, Winston Churchill and Franklin Roosevelt signed the Atlantic Charter to lay out their vision for what a post-Hitler world would look like. They expressed their "faith in life, liberty, independence, and religious freedom, and in the preservation of human rights and justice".[136] Roosevelt was consciously riffing on the Declaration of Independence but with one important update: where Jefferson spoke of "self-evident" rights, Roosevelt admits that these are a matter of "faith". Nevertheless, even at this early stage, the Allies' footing for war was made explicit: faith in human rights.

---

136   Paul Gordon Lauren, *The Evolution of International Human Rights* (University of Pennsylvania Press, 2003), p 149.

This is not to say that the soldiers themselves considered the war in these terms. The American soldier Paul Fussell tells how his fellow GIs "sneered or giggled" at the idea they were on some moral "crusade".[137] The sneering stopped though when they liberated the concentration camps and the scale of the Nazi evil was revealed:

> *"They had seen and smelled the death camps, and now they were able to realize that all along they had been … fighting for something positive, the sacredness of life itself … After the camps, a moral attitude was rampant … The boys' explosive little tour in France had been a crusade after all."*[138]

It is a fearful truth that both Genesis 1 *and* the Holocaust can teach you "the sacredness of life". One teaches the truth positively, the other negatively. Since World War II the negative lesson has often been the louder. We may not know what's up, but we've seen what's down. We're not sure what is good, but we're certain of what is evil. As the historian Alec Ryrie says, "Our modern ethical consensus was summed up by that great philosopher Indiana Jones: 'Nazis! I hate these guys.'"[139]

When the chief architects and executors of the holocaust were tried at Nuremberg (1945–1946) it was vital to

---

137 Alec Ryrie, *What Would Jesus Do? Christian Culture Wars in the Modern West*, Lecture: 14th April 2016. https://www.gresham.ac.uk/lecture/transcript/download/what-would-jesus-do-christian-culture-wars-in-the-modern-west/. Accessed 31st October 2021.

138 As above.

139 Alec Ryrie, "Our Dangerous Devotion to the Second World War", *History Extra*. https://www.historyextra.com/period/20th-century/dangerous-devotion-second-world-war-ww2-west-alec-ryrie/. Accessed 31st October 2021.

judge them against a righteous standard. It would have been unthinkable for the Allies to say of the Third Reich, "Each to their own; who are we to judge?" It would also have been unthinkable for the Allies to say, "Might makes right; we're judging you simply because we won". If justice was to be done, those war criminals had to be tried by a standard that exists high above both the Nazis and the Allies. What standard could fit the bill?

Obviously, in former times, the standard was "God". In the Middle Ages church lawyers would speak of "natural law". An Enlightenment thinker like Jefferson might point to "self-evident" moral truths. But by 1945 those standards were deemed too lofty or too contested. The lawyers at Nuremberg brought the standard right down to earth. They accused the Nazi perpetrators of "crimes against *humanity*" (the language first used regarding slavery a hundred years earlier).

Notice the shift over time. "Humanity" now occupies the place "God" once held. But is "humanity" up to the job? Problems abound.

What do we mean by "humanity" when "humanity" encompasses both the victims *and* the perpetrators? Some humans selflessly hid the Jews during the war, and some ruthlessly gassed them. Both were examples of what "humanity" is capable of. There is kindness in humanity, and there is killing.

So how did we come to the conclusion that "humanity" is, by its nature, anti-fascist? The leading members of the Nazi party did not think so. Heinrich Himmler was clear that we are "but a part of this world".[140] *Certainly the Jew is also a man*, admitted Joseph Goebbels, *but the flea is also an animal*, he continued.[141] If the strong eat the weak in the wild, why not in society too? And why shouldn't the domination of master races over slave races be the norm—a virtue even? Steven Pinker himself ran a thought experiment: if virtue is equated with "sacrifices that benefit one's own group in competition with other groups ... then fascism [is] the ultimate virtuous ideology, and a commitment to human rights the ultimate form of selfishness."[142]

Neither Pinker nor I have the least sympathy for fascism. But the point is to figure out why. And truthfully, it's not because of anything obvious about "humanity" (or, for that matter, "the science"). As the writer T.S. Eliot observed, "If you remove from the word 'human' all that the belief in the supernatural has given to man, you can view him finally as no more than an extremely clever, adaptable, and mischievous little animal."[143] This is a problem.

---

140   Tom Holland, *Dominion* (Little, Brown, 2019), p 537.

141   "Sure, the Jew is also a human being. None of us has every doubted that. But a flea is also an animal—albeit an unpleasant one. Since a flea is not a pleasant animal, we have no duty to defend and protect it, to be of service to it so that it can bite and torment and torture us. Rather, our duty is to make it harmless. The same is true of the Jew." From an early work of propaganda called *The Nazi-Sozi*. https://research.calvin.edu/german-propaganda-archive/nazi-sozi.htm. Accessed 31st October 2021.

142   Steven Pinker, "The False Allure of Group Selection," Edge, 18th June 2012. https://www.edge.org/conversation/steven_pinker-the-false-allure-of-group-selection. Accessed 2nd November 2021.

143   Quoted in Santwana Haldar, *T.S. Eliot: A Twenty-first Century View* (Atlantic Publishers & Distributors, 2005), p 124.

If we're all squabbling apes, then there's no transcendent *justice* in condemning Naziism. What we've done (largely without realising it) has been to clamber up on a stack of Bibles and pronounce the verdict with all the gravity of two millennia of Christian history. But if anyone asks what we're standing on, we obscure the foundations, make transcendent claims for "humanity" and—this has become the chief tactic—point again to the self-evident wickedness of those who oppose human rights. After Auschwitz, such wickedness has become impossible to deny.

When the United Nations was formed (1945) and the Universal Declaration of Human Rights framed (1948), it was done explicitly "in the shadow of evil". Standing against such evil, the declaration uses the same word that Roosevelt and Churchill did, articulating the common *"faith"* that the peoples of the United Nations have in "the dignity and worth of the human person and in the equal rights of men and women'" (emphasis added).[144] It recognises "the inherent dignity and the equal and inalienable rights of all members of the human family", but when addressing the *grounds* for such faith, the preamble essentially points back to that shadow of evil. It argues that "disregard and contempt for human rights have resulted in barbarous acts which have outraged the conscience of mankind". Foundations for the rights on which we stand are not really offered; instead the hellish pit *over there* is pointed out. *It's far better to be here*, says the declaration in effect. This is very true. But we also

---

144 Universal Declaration of Human Rights: https://www.un.org/en/about-us/
universal-declaration-of-human-rights. Accessed 31st October 2021.

need to ask, "What is the nature of *here*? How did we get *here*? And on what basis can we stay?"

It is a common criticism of the declaration that it nails the "What" of human rights yet fails the "Why". It proclaims a vision for human worth and dignity that is completely admirable and largely groundless. This, though, perfectly reflects the position of the average person today:

— Do you believe in human rights?

— *Naturally.*

— Why?

— *... What are you? Some kind of Nazi?*

FLEEING THE PIT AND LOSING OUR WAY
It has been well said that Jesus and Hitler are the two most potent figures in the moral imagination of the West. For 19 centuries we have had a pro-Jesus vision—now we have an anti-Hitler vision. Tom Holland has summarised the new view: "We no longer need the devil because we had Hitler. We no longer needed hell because we had Auschwitz."[145]

What we have *positively* is less clear, but the "new" morality is a case of inverting Naziism (which was itself an inversion of Christianity). If the Nazis pursued racial supremacy, we will pursue racial equality. If the Nazis killed off the weak, we will care for them with large welfare states. (It is often joked that the National Health Service is the real state religion of the UK.) The greatest sins of

---

145 Tom Holland, *How Christianity Gained Dominion* https://www.youtube.com/watch?v=a0xCs2EfiXA (35:06). Accessed 31st October 2021.

the post-war era have become violations of equality and compassion. In psychologist Jonathan Haidt's terms, the two moral foundations valued chiefly by modern liberals are "fairness" and "care" (while other values like loyalty, authority, sanctity and liberty are considered less important or even unintelligible). The sins we really care about are "ism's", especially racism, and the mistreatment of minorities. The slurs that stick are the ones that end in "bigot" or "-phobe" and the predictability of moral arguments descending towards a Nazi comparison is so certain that we consider it a rule.

This is the kind of moral settlement we have come to: a mixture of secularised Christianity and a post-war anti-fascism (which is itself the result of Christian sensibilities). Compassion and equality reign supreme as ideals (often under the titles "diversity" and "inclusion"). These beliefs are precious in themselves, yet they are no longer grounded in the Christian story that first gave them meaning.

In short, a purely secular response to the 20th century has managed to flee from a great pit and yet has lost its way in the process. It inverts Naziism, but it does not thereby restore the original vision. It pursues abstract values (like "humanity", "rights", "freedom", "progress"), but divorced from their source these values prove disconnected, and so do we.

Yet, at the same time, the 20th century gave us a different vision. Running parallel to the secular story was a very different, and very *Christian*, moral example. Let's finish with the hope proclaimed by Martin Luther King.

"I HAVE BEEN TO THE MOUNTAINTOP"

On 3rd April 1968, Martin Luther King gave his "I've been to the mountaintop" speech. He likened himself to Moses, who led the Israelites through the wilderness but died short of the promised land. In his final moments Moses was taken to the top of Mount Nebo to glimpse the "land of milk and honey". King saw himself in those terms—leading a work that would be unfinished in his lifetime but which could not fail because it was God's:

> "Like anybody, I would like to live a long life. Longevity has its place. But I'm not concerned about that now. I just want to do God's will. And He's allowed me to go up to the mountain. And I've looked over. And I've seen the Promised Land. I may not get there with you. But I want you to know tonight, that we, as a people, will get to the Promised Land!"[146]

Here is an unwavering belief in progress. But it's different to the optimism of a Steven Pinker. And it's the reverse of those violent "Leaps Forward" by Mao and the like. The day after King gave this speech he was shot. In his story we see a life expended in sacrificial love, and a hope beyond—and, as such, we see a glimmer of the life of Jesus. There is an arc to our existence. But as it turns out, the arc does not rise up like a rainbow before touching down in the distance. The arc is a long and painful U-shape, plumbing great depths of suffering before rising to justice and peace.

---

146 Martin Luther King Jr. "I've Been To The Mountaintop". https://www. americanrhetoric.com/speeches/mlkivebeentothemountaintop.htm. Accessed 8th October 2021.

King's is an unashamedly biblical vision with an unmistakably Christ-like call. Here is preaching with no concern to soften or secularise the language. And the irony is that such heavenly-mindedness did not detract from King's broad appeal—it was the source of it. In truth, all talk of human rights has Christian sources (whether they are declared or not). King was simply speaking equality's mother tongue, and it struck the Christianised hearts of his hearers with unnatural force. It still speaks if we have ears to hear it. And we need to hear it.

Western society has splintered into ever narrower identity groupings, with less and less shared narrative to bind us together. When conflict arises, we have fewer social and spiritual resources to help us forgive and reconcile. The secular river is running dry. Nevertheless, there is hope. Ironically, progress can be found in going back—back to the source.

9. THE KINGDOM WITHOUT THE KING

"I can't breathe."

— George Floyd, 25 May 2020

He said it 27 times in nine minutes. George Floyd's plea to an indifferent police officer kneeling on the back of his neck was desperately familiar. "I can't breathe" were the last words of many others including Eric Garner, another black man killed in a police encounter in 2014. But the words and the context of Floyd's death had a resonance that went deeper still.

The cell-phone footage rippled out from Minneapolis so that, within days, there were thousands of protests not only around the United States but in Germany, the UK, France, Mexico, Australia, Israel, Southeast Asia and parts of Africa. This prompted Joe Biden to claim that Floyd's death was having a greater worldwide impact than Martin Luther King's had had. More than half a century after King's assassination, the comparisons were not difficult to make. These were black men unjustly killed by white aggressors, and their deaths struck right at the heart of America's claim to be founded on inalienable rights and equality. King had called the Declaration of Independence a "promissory note", unfulfilled in his day. 52 years later protestors took to the streets—at least

15 million of them in the US alone—marching, toppling statues and raising their voices to demand that the promise be realised.

The fact that all this was occurring three months into a global pandemic reminds us that there are human values that eclipse even those of life and health. It turns out that we are not merely biological creatures seeking safety or capitalist consumers seeking comfort. We are moral agents seeking righteousness. Martin Luther King was correct to speak of a "moral universe". That's where we live. And that's why we all care so much about justice (even if we disagree about how such justice should be achieved).

But of all the events that might have lit the fuse, why did Floyd's death affect us so profoundly? In a sense this whole book is an answer to that question. Floyd's death gripped us because our moral universe has been birthed out of similar pains. It was an echo of what happened on a hill outside Jerusalem two millennia before: an unarmed victim of oppression; an uncaring authority; a public and humiliating death; and a world that came to see the virtue of the victim and the tyranny of the oppressor. Even Floyd's cry, "I can't breathe", could have been placed on Christ's own lips. As author and tech entrepreneur Antonio García Martínez has said, "The Western mind is like a tuning fork calibrated to one frequency: the Christ story. Hit it with the right Christ figure, and it'll just hum deafeningly in resonance."[147]

---

147 Antonio García Martínez, "The Christ with a thousand faces". https://www.thepullrequest.com/p/the-christ-with-a-thousand-faces. Accessed 26th January 2022.

Floyd came to be seen as just such a Christ figure by many—even if they might never have acknowledged this as such. He was quickly identified as a kind of martyr and saint. Religious responses were everywhere. Street art put a halo above Floyd's head, crowds were led in communal acts of repentance, and they confessed together "creedal" truths about race and equality.

One prominent act, "taking the knee", goes back, at least in part, to the very heart of our story of freedom and progress. The emblem of the abolitionists, the Wedgwood anti-slavery medallion, depicted an enslaved man kneeling while asking, "Am I not a man and a brother?" The right of every person to equal humanity before the law was bound up with their equal humility before God. Kneeling was also a compelling image in the civil-rights movement. In a famous photograph from 1965, King is leading many protesters in prayer as they are about to be jailed. All are kneeling. There are certainly other influences on "taking the knee"—these currents and trends swirl around us, with the sources not always clear. Yet we are swept along nonetheless.

In 2020 these gestures, slogans and movements came together with remarkable force. They carried—and were carried upon—streams of moral and political sentiment so powerful that they are best described as religious. More particularly, they are Christian in their source.

And it's not just those who marched who found themselves swept up. Those who questioned the protests were appealing to Christian convictions too. Keir Starmer wanted the Edward Colston statue down but via democratic means (a process assuming the equal voice of all). Many supported the protests but emphasised King's methods of *non-violent* resistance. Others worried that some anti-racist movements were re-racialising the discourse and reversing King's teaching that people should be judged *not* "by the color of their skin but by the content of their character".

On and on it goes; back and forth the arguments run, with one set of Christian-ish instincts clashing with another. Whether people realise it or not, these culture wars involve devout believers hurling Bible verses at one another—they've just forgotten the references.

Perhaps, though, the days of Christian influence are over in the West—or, at least, severely numbered. It might be granted that Christianity has profoundly shaped our culture up to now, but haven't we now lost touch with our traditional roots? This is our next "Hang On".

HANG ON: ISN'T CHRISTIAN INFLUENCE OVER IN THE WEST?

In October 2019, a British court ruled against David Mackereth in a case that epitomises our modern culture wars. In a job interview Mackereth, a doctor with 30 years of experience, wished to reserve the right not to refer to, in his words, "a 6ft-tall bearded man as 'madam'".[148] When he was not employed, he claimed he was discriminated against because he made known that his beliefs were based

---

148 "David Mackereth: Christian doctor loses trans beliefs case", BBC News, https://www.bbc.co.uk/news/uk-england-birmingham-49904997. Accessed 31st October 2021.

on Genesis 1:27—the verse we've referenced more than any other in this book. For Mackereth, the belief that "God created mankind in his own image ... male and female" was foundational. When the case went to court, the ruling went against Mackereth. In particular, the doctor's belief in Genesis 1:27 was singled out by the judge as "incompatible with human dignity". And so the verse that lies at the roots of "human dignity" was condemned in a judgment that very much calls to mind the image of a culture sawing at the branch of the tree on which it is perched.

So has the tide of Christian influence finally gone out? That kind of imagery has long been reflected in the language of conservative and religious types who lament the retreat of faith in the public square. The 19th-century poet Matthew Arnold once spoke of the "long, withdrawing roar" of the "Sea of Faith", leaving us with "neither joy, nor love, nor light":

> "The Sea of Faith
> Was once, too, at the full, and round earth's shore
> Lay like the folds of a bright girdle furled.
> But now I only hear
> Its melancholy, long, withdrawing roar,
> Retreating, to the breath
> Of the night-wind, down the vast edges drear
> And naked shingles of the world."[149]

If Arnold could write this in 1851 (when half of England was in church on a Sunday), what would he make of today?[150]

---

149 "Dover Beach" by Matthew Arnold, https://www.poetryfoundation.org/poems/43588/dover-beach. Accessed 30th October 2021.

150 10 million of Britain's population of 18 million attended church in 1851. This

What should we make of it when church attendance in England is around 6%, and the biblical foundations of society are sometimes publicly condemned?[151]

Well, it's worth remembering that tides go out, but they also come in. There have been many "long, withdrawing roars" in church history and equally many extraordinary surges. Tides do not go out for ever. But there is another way to develop the "sea of faith" analogy: the power of the water is in evidence no matter what its current level is. The terrain at low tide has been shaped by the ocean as surely as the beach at high tide. In other words, Christianity is still powerfully at work in all these contemporary trends, and those both inside and outside the church should be aware of the dynamics. Let's consider them in the Mackereth case.

In 2019 the beliefs of Dr Mackereth, a committed Christian, ran up against transgender ideology, but both outlooks were dependent, in their own ways, on Christian assumptions. In particular, the first three values considered by this book—equality, compassion and consent—were driving the arguments. It's just that, in the case of certain transgender advocates, those values have been divorced from the Christian story and then combined in a new way. Let's examine both: the divorce and the recombination.

---

was split between about 5 million in the Church of England and 5 million in the remaining denominations. "Religious Worship in England and Wales, Census of Great Britain, 1851", https://archive.org/details/censusgreatbrit00manngoog. Accessed 30th October 2021.

151   P. Brierley, *UK Church Statistics 3, 2018 Edition*, (ABCD Publishers, 2017).

When *equality* is divorced from the Christian story, it risks becoming a radical individualism. Ancient people considered their identity in collective ways, and individuality got lost in the shuffle. We have the opposite danger. We consider our society as a loose association of individuals who each have equal rights before the law. It can become very atomistic: I begin my thinking with myself and my identity. Where, in other cultures, I would look outwards to discover my identity, in our culture I look inwards. Where other cultures major on responsibilities, we major on rights. No wonder a sense of community suffers. No wonder *all* forms of institutional affiliations are tanking across the board (not just church attendance).

In Christianity the principle is that all sit equally at the same table. The modern goal is for all to climb equally high up their own ladders. Where the Bible says, "There is neither Jew nor Gentile, neither slave nor free, nor is there male and female, for you are all one in Christ Jesus" (Galatians 3:28), 21st-century Westerners now finish that sentence, "... for you are all individuals". Or, worse, "... for you are all interchangeable". At that point, the distance travelled from the Scriptural truth is immense.

When *compassion* is divorced from the Christian story, it risks generating "competitive victimhood". This is the name sociologists have given for the way victim status can be quickly claimed to gain an advantage. In Christianity, the Victim, Jesus, suffered redemptively and offers dignity and hope to the oppressed. The danger nowadays is that our chief desire is not to honour and help victims but to become them. Where virtue was once the cultivation of a great heart, nowadays we seek to demonstrate a thin skin.

And with so many claiming victimisation—a great many of them having genuine grievances—we lack a richer moral vision to arbitrate. The clashes between feminists (or religious minorities) on the one hand and trans-rights activists on the other demonstrate the point. Here we see claims made on both sides about the protection of the oppressed. Which should take precedence, when, and on what grounds? To answer those questions we need a far more robust understanding of the meaning of gender, bodies, personhood and community. And we need more tools at our disposal than an insistence on "my rights", the retelling of "my suffering" and some caps-locked tweets reminding people, "IT'S THE 21ST CENTURY FOR GOODNESS SAKE."

When sexual *consent* is divorced from the Christian story, it risks reducing sex to something far less than the Christian vision. It detaches consent—a vital component of the sexual relationship—from other values, like commitment. It also risks detaching sex from a richer story about its meaning. It can naively assume that sex involves uncomplicated choices regarding a leisure activity. In reality, power differentials, both social and physical, are always present, and sex is woven into the fabric of our bodies, our personal relationships and our societal structures. As the individualists that we are, we are minded to view sex as a matter for private individuals making a private transaction, but our identities, our bodies, our lives and our sexual choices are intimately connected to marriage, children, family, biology and the wider community. Consent is vital, but it is not a sufficient foundation for sexual ethics.

Now mix these three abstracted values together in a certain way and you have a heady brew: the power of the individual; the power of the minority; and the power of personal choice, especially in sexual matters. These are foundational beliefs for transgender ideology. For the trans-rights activist it adds up to this: I have an absolute right to self-identify, independent of culture or biology, and, as a minority, my choice must be honoured. Obviously this ideology is not Christian, but it emerges from strongly held convictions that would be utterly inconceivable without Christianity.

On the other side, David Mackereth has his own Christian foundations: the rights to religious liberty, to freedom of speech and to freedom of conscience; science (in particular, biological definitions of sex); and the scriptural authority which grounds our equality in the first place (Genesis 1:27!). And so what we have in this 2019 tribunal is a clash between traditional and secularised versions of some foundationally *Christian* values. What was alarming was not so much that the ruling went against Mackereth—in culture wars some battles are won and some are lost. What was alarming was the reason given. The judge ruled that Genesis 1 itself was the problem. As Spencer Klavan has said, calling the image of God "incompatible with human dignity is akin to insisting that seeds are incompatible with flowers, or grain with bread."[152] It is to condemn the roots of the tree, even as you depend on the fruits it has yielded.

---

152 "Going Off the Rails", Spencer Klavan, Clermont Review of Books, Winter 2020, https://claremontreviewofbooks.com/going-off-the-rails. Accessed 20th October 2021.

Such a trend towards ever-increasing secularisation is not, therefore, a sustainable strategy. It is, as we will see, a recipe for fracture and not freedom. But one thing it reveals is the inescapable influence of Christianity. Even as Genesis is condemned, it is condemned for "Christian" reasons.

The tide is certainly out in terms of Christianity's explicit influence on Western culture. But the terrain has been shaped by a "sea of faith" far deeper and more enduring than our current cultural moment. And as we witness the fear, confusion, and tribalism of our post-Christian age, there are reasons for people within *and beyond* the church to wish for the tide to turn.

"SOMEONE IS WRONG ON THE INTERNET"

In recent years cavernous fault lines have opened up in Western society. Some blame catastrophes like 9/11, the financial crash of 2007, and the COVID pandemic. Others blame polarising social media and/or a polarising US President. But no matter where we line up on these cultural divides, the values to which we appeal largely remain. Whether you agree or disagree with "taking the knee", or toppling statues, or "black lives matter", or Black Lives Matter, or defunding the police, or reparations for slavery, or a thousand other questions stirred by the death of George Floyd, the fundamentals remain. We still believe in the WEIRD values at the heart of this book:

- Consider equality: once, steep moral hierarchies were the norm; now we want to root out inequalities wherever we find them.

- Consider compassion: once, pity for the undeserving was considered a weakness; now we consider it a virtue.

- Consider consent: once, powerful men could possess the bodies of whomever they pleased; now we name this as the abuse that it is.

- Consider enlightenment: once, education was a luxury for rich men; now we consider it a necessity for all.

- Consider science: once, knowledge of the natural world was based on the assertions of authorities; now we hold the powerful to account and we seek to test such claims against objective standards.

- Consider freedom: once, it was assumed that certain classes of people could be enslaved; now we consider that idea a kind of "blasphemy".

- Consider progress: once, history was thought of as a descent from a golden age; now we feel that the arc of history bends, or should bend, towards justice.

These are our credal convictions, and, by and large, we are a society of believers. So thoroughly do we assent to these values that we rarely notice how weird they are, or how WEIRD we are for holding them. But with these morals in place, we have found that we can discard institutional Christianity *yet carry on with the moralising*. In fact, the moralising, far from receding, is coming to the fore. This has been a shock to many.

We used to think that "without God ... all things are permitted".[153] That was a line the novelist Fyodor Dostoevsky put into the mouth of one of his characters over 140 years ago. Many have believed this sentiment whether they are inside or outside the church. It seems logical that without God and without the constraints of organised religion, society might enjoy greater freedom. It turns out we enjoy finger-wagging even more. Without God it's not that everything is permitted—instead, everything is preachy. Painfully so.

If anyone blasphemes our WEIRD values (or if anyone can be portrayed as blaspheming them), we "cancel" them— that is, we ostracise them socially and professionally. This is really a modern form of "excommunication" for modern kinds of "heretics". And while our modern "inquisitions" are less fatal than the old ones (for which we give great thanks), they are also much more widespread. The process is described in detail by Jon Ronson in his book, *So You've Been Publicly Shamed*. The storms of public outrage that sweep through social media mean that thousands at a time are able to take on the roles of judge, jury and executioner. So while the person accused of "blaspheming" is buried beneath the barrage, the multitudes who participate in the pile-on get lost in the crowd: "The snowflake never needs to feel responsible for the avalanche".[154] The role of inquisitor has been democratised. Anyone can join the Twitchfork mob, and everyone is invited—continually. But if anyone can participate in the pile on, it's difficult

---

153   Fyodor Dostoevsky, *The Brothers Karamazov*, translated by Richard Pevear and Larissa Volokhonsky (North Point Press, 1990), p 589.

154   Jon Ronson, *So You've Been Publicly Shamed* (Pan Macmillan, 2015), p 53.

to escape the feeling that, equally, anyone could be the next target.

There are many factors at play in what has been dubbed "cancel culture". Certainly, social media plays a role in the ways it turbocharges our outrage. But the existence of the outrage in the first place is a matter of the heart. It arises when enlightened souls feel compelled to enlighten others who are lost in the dark. It's fundamentally an evangelistic zeal—there's a preacher inside us all. You don't need to be a churchgoer to feel it.

One of the more perfect depictions of online culture is a cartoon which shows a man angrily hammering at his keyboard while his partner says, "Are you coming to bed?" "I can't," he replies. "Someone is <u>wrong</u> on the internet."[155] The man is, for want of a better word, a missionary. He is enlightened, and he wants to shine that light into dark places. He feels a burning passion to proclaim the truth and liberate those who are bound by lies. The internet did not make him like this; it merely helped him to spread the word. His need to be right and to share that rightness with others goes very deep. Place him together with others who are similarly convinced of their rightness and you will get accusations flying with a strength of feeling, a righteous indignation and a desire to banish the blasphemer that could well be described as "religious". It is the worst version of the Christian instinct towards "enlightenment". And it lacks the very heart of what Christianity has to offer: *forgiveness*.

---

155 "Duty Calls," https://xkcd.com/386/. Accessed 3rd November 2021.

THE CURSE OF SEMI-CHRISTIANITY

In *The Madness of Crowds*, author Douglas Murray speaks of the moral certainties that nowadays are turned into moralising crusades. He devotes a chapter to the subject of forgiveness, seeing it as a lost art in modern life. As a society we have, it seems, kept Christianity's sense of sin but forgotten entirely about salvation. We are all "guilt" and no "grace".

> *"As one of the consequences of the death of God, [the 19th century philosopher] Nietzsche foresaw that people could find themselves stuck in cycles of Christian theology with no way out. Specifically that people would inherit the concepts of guilt, sin and shame but would be without the means of redemption which the Christian religion also offered. Today we do seem to live in a world where ... guilt and shame are more at hand than ever, and where we have no means whatsoever of redemption."*[156]

This is inevitable. The Western experiment has been an attempt to secularise Christianity. As Johnny Cash once sang, "They say they want the kingdom, but they don't want God in it." In order to pursue the kingdom without the King, we have had to dethrone the *person* of Christ and install abstract values instead. The problem should be obvious: persons can forgive you; values cannot. Values can only judge you.

Such values were never ultimate in Christianity. Christian morals have always been the morals *to a story*. In the

---

156 Douglas Murray, *The Madness of Crowds* (Bloomsbury Continuum, 2019), p 182.

West today we have ditched the story, anonymised the Hero and kept the morals—and now we wonder why our culture splinters under a million angry accusations. The kingdom without the King is not a place of liberation so much as a place of judgment. But in this democratic republic, we are all the judges, and we are all the judged. We desperately need a *person* above and beyond the values—a person who does not simply expect our best but who forgives our worst.

When considering the seven values of the last seven chapters, we might nod them through as fine ideas (we can't help but do that). But who can claim to have fulfilled them? Who has never used their power to the detriment of another? Who has never acted as though their life was of greater value than those of the people around them? Who has always shown compassion to those who are in need? Certainly not me. And if you're honest enough to admit it, not you either.

As we tear down Edward Colston, how can we do so without inviting similar scrutiny of our own culture, our own complicity, our own crimes. We ought to ask ourselves, "How will history judge us?" Or, to put the question in a biblical frame, "How will God judge us?"

The Old Testament psalm asks, "If you, LORD, kept a record of sins, Lord, who could stand?" (Psalm 130:3). It expects the answer "no one". Not Colston and not me. Wonderfully, though, the psalm continues, "But with you there is forgiveness" (v 4). History cannot forgive us but only judge us. Values cannot forgive us but only judge us. But with God there is forgiveness. He is above the values. He is free to treat us better than our law-breaking deserves. In fact, he promises to forgive us when we come to him with our guilt.

This is the heart of the Christian story we have been telling. When Jesus came, he described himself as a spiritual doctor. As such he was drawn not to the fit but to the failing:

> "It is not the healthy who need a doctor, but those who are ill. I have not come to call the righteous, but sinners." (Mark 2:17)

Christ presents himself not as a moral policeman but as a spiritual healer. He comes not to accuse but to acquit, if only we will own our need for it. Here is the heart of Christian faith: admitting our sin and knowing Christ's forgiveness. For those who know that they are like Edward Colston—a mixture of some goodness and much badness, with more than enough corruption to condemn them—this is wonderful news. The Doctor will see us. He will forgive us and, having forgiven us, he will teach us to forgive others.

At the heart of the daily prayer that Christ teaches his followers is the plea "Forgive us our sins as we forgive those who sin against us" (Matthew 6:9-15, NLV). This is what the Bible means by living a life "under grace" (Romans 6:14). To be "under grace" is to receive the stream of undeserved mercy flowing from above and to share it with others.

The alternative, biblically speaking, is to live "under law". If "grace" is a flow from above, "law" is a ladder we must climb—some are higher, some are lower, and all feel judged. This is the nature of secularised "Christianity". Our abstract values are laws. And when laws are the air we breathe, our atmosphere is judgment. It's suffocating.

In the 19th century the preacher Charles Spurgeon warned about the dangers of semi-Christianity. He said, "Be half a Christian and you shall have enough religion to make you miserable".[157] He was concerned for individual churchgoers who knew enough of the Bible to understand its good advice but not its good news. They appreciated Christ's standards but not Christ's story. They therefore knew the laws but not the love—the guilt but not the grace. This did not leave them halfway happy but downright despondent.

What Spurgeon witnessed in individuals we can see in society. We have a kind of semi-Christianity in the West, and it's enough to make us miserable. In the next chapter we will consider the way forward: a return to the real thing.

---

157 Charles Spurgeon, "The Foundation and Its Seal—a Sermon for the Times" https://www.ccel.org/ccel/spurgeon/sermons31.xxxix.html. Accessed 31st October 2021. It goes on, "Be wholly a Christian and your joy shall be full!"

10. CHOOSE YOUR MIRACLE

"I'm amazed at my own belief, and I don't understand it."

— Jordan Peterson, 2021

We met Jordan Peterson back in chapter 2. He is a best-selling author, a psychology professor and a successful YouTuber. For years he has maintained a studied agnosticism about his faith. When asked whether he believes in God, he repeatedly states that he doesn't like the question but that he acts as though God exists. In 2017 he began a series of surprisingly popular biblical lectures walking slowly through the stories of Genesis and bringing out their psychological significance. As he has written:

> *"The Bible is, for better or worse, the foundational document of western civilization ... Its careful, respectful study can reveal things to us about what we believe and how we do and should act that can be discovered in almost no other manner."*[158]

This has made many uncomfortable. When he debated with the atheist Sam Harris in four popular events in 2018, the fear was expressed that Peterson, and others

---

158 Jordan Peterson, *12 Rules For Life* (Random House Canada, 2018), p 104.

like him, were merely "Jesus smuggling". It's the idea that Peterson is concealing his true Christian intentions, masking them with a veneer of scientific and intellectual respectability. Underneath the secular-speak, they fear, he is trying to sneak Jesus into our hearts and minds.

If you've been following the argument of this book, you will recognise the tactic. But you will also recognise that it's not Jordan Peterson who is Jesus-smuggling. Western civilisation is a vast, centuries-long exercise in Jesus-smuggling. At first it was overt; now it's covert. Today, whether we're talking about rights, or "diversity and inclusion", or the miracle of scientific intelligibility, or humanitarian ideals, or a moral universe bending towards justice, we are complicit in an immense Bible-trafficking operation. When we speak of humanity, history, freedom, progress, or enlightenment values, with the significance now attached to those terms, we are carrying on a Christian conversation. The language and logic are unmistakable even if at points we've learnt to modify our vocabulary.

It's not just Peterson who is pointing out the Christian sources of our values. In this book we have already heard from writers such as Larry Siedentop, Tom Holland, Rodney Stark, Kyle Harper, Joseph Henrich and others. None of them are Christians, but all of them are noticing how comprehensively we have been shaped by Christian history. And what these writers are engaged in is the opposite of Jesus-smuggling—they're exposing the Christianity which has already been smuggled into every corner of our world. Peterson and others are outing the true Bible bootleggers: the secularists.

But even as Peterson acknowledges the foundation of our values, doing so has also set him on a personal journey. The opening quotation from this chapter is taken from an interview with Christian YouTuber Jonathan Pageau in 2021. Peterson wept as he admitted being drawn, almost against his will, towards Christian faith.

Yet the fascinating part was his reasoning. In leaning towards Christian faith and away from a purely secular account of the world, he recognised that *both* positions—the Christian *and* the secular—were faith positions. Both involve "impossible" assertions.

> *"I've got the choice of believing two impossible things. I can either believe that the world is constituted so that God took on flesh and was crucified and rose three days later or I can believe that human beings invented this unbelievably preposterous story that has stretched into every atom of culture. And it isn't obvious to me that the second hypothesis is any easier to believe than the first. Because the more you investigate the manifestations of the story of Christ the more insanely complicated and far-reaching it becomes."*[159]

It is "impossible" to believe that God took on humanity, died and rose again. But it's also "impossible" to believe that this "preposterous story" has reached into every facet of modern life to transform it utterly. A Christian believes the first impossible truth but a secularist is left with the second. We all have "impossible" faith positions then.

---

159 Jordan B. Peterson Podcast S4 E8, 1st March 2021: https://youtu.be/2rAqVmZwqZM. Accessed 1st November 2021.

How should we break the deadlock? Well, it's worth remembering that the second impossible thing—the enduring influence of the Jesus story—has in fact happened: *a man on a cross has made our Western world.* At this point, even the staunchest rationalist is left with an absurdity. But the Christian can come along with an explanation: "The reason a man on a cross has made our world is because he is our Maker—God himself."

Peterson's story is far from over and far from a straight line. Who knows where his journey will take him? This is not about claiming him for "Team Jesus" nor implying that he will inevitably gravitate towards church. The point is simply to acknowledge some of his key insights. He shows us that everyone is a believer, everyone has absurdities to own, and everyone must account for the incomparable impact of Jesus Christ.

There is, of course, a natural response to all this. It takes seriously the points made above, but it says, "Fine. We came from Christianity, but so what? Our values had to come from *somewhere*. None of this makes Christianity *inevitable* or *true*."

In the next section I want to respond to this by underlining two extraordinary features of the Jesus revolution which convince me that its source is ultimately from above rather than below—from God and not simply from human developments. First, it has fulfilled predictions, and, second, it has defied expectations. In all this I invite you to consider that Christianity is not a "natural" development, but something *super*natural.

PREDICTING THE PECULIAR

From beginning to end, the Bible predicts and proclaims an extraordinary development in world affairs: the victory of the Victim.

First, the Old Testament. These books could also be called "the Jewish Scriptures" or "the Hebrew Bible". Even the latest of these books was written hundreds of years before the first Christmas, yet they speak of a coming Messiah ("anointed one") with a startling beauty, unity and clarity.

In Genesis 3, as soon as Adam and Eve plunge the world into ruin ("the fall"), they hear a prophecy of redemption in which the offspring of the woman (a promised Saviour) will crush the head of the serpent (the bringer of death and chaos). Yet even as the Saviour deals the death blow, his heel will be struck (Genesis 3:15). He would defeat evil through suffering.

As Genesis continues, the question rolls on: who will bear this promised child? We meet Abraham (father of the Jewish nation), his offspring Isaac, Isaac's offspring Jacob, and then Jacob's twelve sons. The promise is being narrowed to a single family line. By the end of the Bible's first book, we hear Jacob's prophecy about his son Judah:

> "The sceptre will not depart from Judah, nor the ruler's staff from between his feet, until he to whom it belongs shall come and the obedience of the nations shall be his." (Genesis 49:10)

Judah will father Israel's royal tribe, and yet each king will be only a throne-warmer for the universal Ruler. One day the golden child will come. And this King from the line of little old Judah will be a King for the whole world.

Let's jump forwards to the prophets (leaping over dozens of similar prophecies and several hundred years of history), and listen in as these divinely appointed messengers take up the theme of the promised birth:

> "For to us a child is born,
>   to us a son is given,
>   and the government will be on his shoulders
>   And he will be called
>   Wonderful Counsellor, Mighty God,
>   Everlasting Father, Prince of Peace.
>   Of the greatness of his government and peace
>   there will be no end.
>   He will reign on David's throne
>   and over his kingdom,
>   establishing and upholding it
>   with justice and righteousness
>   from that time on and for ever." (Isaiah 9:6-7)

The promised child will be the "Mighty God", taking charge of his own creation and bringing an unstoppable reign of peace. His kingdom will increase continually from the time of his birth "and for ever". This is not usual for kingdoms. Everyone knows that kingdoms rise and fall—certainly the Israelites did. They endured the cruelties of the Babylonians, the Persians, the Greeks, and, in time, the Romans. But while the British Museum displays the scattered remains of those mighty empires, the kingdom of the Messiah continues to grow, just as predicted. It's a theme taken up by another prophet: Daniel.

In one vision the 6th-century prophet Daniel pictures an impressive statue made of four materials representing the oppressive kingdoms mentioned above. But he also prophesies an unlikely victor over imperial power. "A rock ... cut out, but not by human hands" strikes the statue, destroying it. The stone then grows to become "a huge mountain" and fills "the whole earth" (Daniel 2:34, 35). In chapter 7 Daniel reprises the same themes. This time the empires are represented by beasts brutalising God's people, and yet there comes one who is not beastly at all, who is described as being "like a son of man" (Daniel 7:13). Against the monstrous forces of worldly might, what hope does this "son of man" have? Yet the son of man turns out to be God's "right-hand man", and through his *humanity* (not his cruelty) he overcomes the imperial powers:

"He was given authority, glory and sovereign power; all nations and peoples of every language worshipped him. His dominion is an everlasting dominion that will not pass away, and his kingdom is one that will never be destroyed." (Daniel 7:14)

No wonder messianic expectation was at fever pitch in the 1st century. Israel was in the grip of that fourth beastly power, Rome. It was time for the promised Saviour to come. When Jesus arrived on the scene, he stepped confidently into these expectations. He responded to many titles: "Messiah" (Matthew 16:16), "Son of David" (Luke 18:38), and "Son of God" (John 11:27). He also accepted worship as "Lord and ... God" (John 20:28). But the title he used of himself more than any other was "Son of Man".

He certainly carried himself as though he had that long-prophesied "everlasting dominion". He was a penniless preacher without a scrap of earthly power, and yet he considered his words to be eternally authoritative (Matthew 24:35). He never wrote a book or founded a school, but he considered his judgment to be everlastingly decisive (Matthew 25:31-34). He never entered politics or religious orders or the military, but he was confident that the movement he founded would be like a pinch of yeast which works its way into the whole batch of dough—the whole world (Matthew 13:33). Likewise, he predicted that his teaching would be like the smallest seed that ends up growing into the largest tree (v 31-32). From small beginnings his kingdom would expand to fill the earth. Intriguingly Jesus adds the detail of birds who find themselves perching in the tree's branches (v 32). The last time Jesus mentioned birds, they were pecking at the seed—opposing the growth (v 4). Now they find their home within it. Such is the surprising and inexorable expansion of the Jesus movement, and all of it was predicted long in advance.

Yet Jesus did not merely predict that his movement would triumph; he predicted how. Remarkably, it would be through the victory of the Victim. In Matthew 16 Jesus proclaims two certainties: he will assuredly die a violent death, and his movement will assuredly conquer the world. The church, he says, will expand far into enemy territory: even "the gates of Hades will not overcome it" (Matthew 16:13-18). Gates, of course, are static. The church is not. The image is of the church advancing irresistibly, breaking down the gates of hell, plundering the kingdom of darkness, rescuing captives for the kingdom of light. And while, in the ensuing ages, there will be great hardship, Jesus declares—in his provincial northern accent—that the good news of his kingdom "will be preached in the whole world" (Matthew 24:14).

Within days of this declaration, Christ is hanging on a Roman cross in God-forsaken agony. It looks nothing like a triumph. Yet even in this moment, Jesus' confidence is unshaken. His dying words, "It is finished", are a cry of victory (John 19:30). He considers himself to be accomplishing his life's work. In laying down his life on the cross, he is taking on himself the sin and guilt of his people. He is doing what love does: entering the world of his beloved to shoulder their burdens. The Judge is judged in our place, so that we, the guilty, may go free. Jesus is "the Lamb of God, who takes away the sin of the world" (John 1:29).

But is this really a victory? It's not if the Victim remains in the grave.

Three days later, so the Gospels tell us, Jesus rose up bodily and appeared to his disciples, alive again. And he gave to his ragtag group of followers a global assignment: they must go into all the world and make the nations into followers of the Jewish Messiah (Matthew 28:18-20). This is what Genesis promised, this is what Jesus commanded, and this is what his movement has been accomplishing ever since.

When we see the triumph of the Jesus revolution, we are not simply looking back at a curious twist in the tale of world history. The twist was foretold. The victory of the Victim was prophesied in the Hebrew Bible and proclaimed by Christ himself long before there was any earthly plausibility regarding its fulfilment.

But perhaps that sounds all too suspicious for you. Here is our final "Hang On".

HANG ON: WAS THE JESUS STORY FABRICATED?

We have been putting quite a bit of store by Matthew's Gospel in the arguments above. Perhaps Matthew and the other Gospel writers are not to be trusted. Perhaps they took strands of the historical Jesus and wove them together with the extraordinary prophecies of old to create a fabulous tale—one to take the world by storm. It's worth pressing into that possibility. If nothing else, doing so reveals the scale of the project.

Imagine the writers' room as someone commissions the authors of the Gospels:

> "Ok, Matthew, Mark, Luke and John, I have a job for you. I know you've had no training or prior experience, but we need you to write the most influential works in literature. As for the timing, we'll have to move on this unfortunately. It would have been better to wait a couple of centuries before inventing our legends; that way none of Christ's contemporaries could contradict our story. But we are where we are: the apostle Paul has forced the pace, writing his letters to churches around the Mediterranean. He's been preaching Jesus as the promised Messiah and, heaven knows why, but all these people have believed in 'God on a cross'. The story

seems to be working, so now we need you to fill in the details. Please can you write the origins story for our Hero? Paul's letters gave the bare bones; we want you to put warm flesh on them. Are you up to it?

"It won't be easy. We need this to be the life and times of the greatest figure in human history—God but also man, sinless but fully alive, pure but with profound depths, the Judge of the world but with bottomless compassion, the fulfilment of all Jewish hopes but with a global appeal, a man in time but a man for all times. We need a Hero with heart-melting kindness yet steely determination. We need him blasting the self-righteous and befriending sinners. We need sublime ethical teaching to fall from his lips—the kind that builds civilisations. We need extraordinary miracles from him—the kind that would have been noticed (and could therefore be contradicted) by the generation to which you're writing. We need a credible narrative arc whereby he remains impeccably righteous but is nonetheless condemned as a blasphemer. And we need it all to stand up to scrutiny: scriptural, theological, geographic, linguistic, literary and historical. It needs to be believable both near and far, now and later, for those who've lived through these times and for all generations to come. Got it? Now get to work!"

This is why Jordan Peterson finds it so difficult to believe that "human beings invented this unbelievably preposterous story". It is, in his words, an "impossible" task. When you read the Gospels for yourself, you begin to ask, along with Bible scholar Peter Williams, "Which genius comes up with this?"[160] There is genius here. There is enough genius in the Jesus story to remake the world. But we need to ask: does the genius reside in the authors, or have the authors basically reported the genius of their Hero, Jesus? Both options are somewhat "miraculous", but one of them involves a Miracle Maker who can explain the feat.

LIFE FROM THE DEAD

Let's review where we've been so far. From Genesis onwards "the victory of the Victim" has been predicted. According to the prophecies, the promised one would defeat evil at great cost to himself. Then Jesus shows up in the middle of history as "the Lamb of God"—the willing Victim to be sacrificed for our sins. The rest of the New Testament proclaims the unlikely victory of this Victim. But there's one more stop on our rapid tour of the Scriptures.

The Bible ends with a heavenly vision of a "Lamb, looking as if it had been slain", on the throne of the universe (Revelation 5:6). When taken literally, the image is absurd, obviously, but such is the style of Revelation, the Bible's final book. It uses pictorial language to present its vision of reality—both what is now and what is yet to come. Once you understand the representations, the meaning is understood. Jesus is "the Lamb at the centre of the throne" (7:17). He is the Victim who, *because he was sacrificed*, is at the heart of the Bible's understanding of God. He is the Ruler of heaven and earth. And the promise of Revelation

---

160 Peter J. Williams & Bart Ehrman, *The Story of Jesus: Are the Gospels Historically Reliable?* https://www.youtube.com/watch?v=ZuZPPGvF_2I. Accessed 1st November 2021.

is that this "Lamb" will end up being worshipped by "a great multitude that no one could count, from every nation, tribe, people and language" (v 9).

These are absolutely extraordinary beliefs, and it's hard to decide which of them is the most extraordinary: that the one sacrificed on the cross should be identified as God; that he has triumphed *through* his bloody sacrifice; or that the whole world will come to see the glory of the bloodied God? The tiny Jesus movement of the 1st century embraced every aspect of this "unbelievably preposterous story", to use Peterson's phrase, and yet it "has stretched into every atom of culture". The triumph of the Jesus-movement has defied all human expectations.

Whatever your views about miracles, everyone must grapple with an extraordinary "life-from-the-dead" occurrence in the 1st century. No one who had seen Jesus' followers on the day after his death—dejected, scared, leaderless and hiding for fear of the authorities—would have expected their movement to shape history in the way that it has. Something was unleashed on the world 20 centuries ago such that, from an ignominious death, life has burst out.

A scientific analogy may help. Physicists first theorised about a Big Bang because they observed an expanding universe. It made them wonder about the origins of the expansion, and they reckoned that, at some point in the past, there was cosmic inflation, a force unleashed, a "Big Bang".

This book has been observing a different kind of expansion—the expansion of the Jesus revolution which has "stretched into every atom of culture". If we trace it back to its origins, we come to the 1st century. Something happened. An incredible power was unleashed: a primal force. And Christians put a name to this "Big Bang". They claim, in line with the Old and New Testaments, that it was the resurrection of Jesus that birthed the expansion we have witnessed. The Victim has been victorious over the course of history because the Victim was victorious *in* history: three days after his crucifixion, Jesus rose from the dead. The tomb was empty; his followers reported encounters with him; and the period of history we have surveyed in this book was set in motion.

The resurrection of Jesus is undeniably a miracle. But it's not a miracle that adds to the absurdity of your world. The resurrection explains what would otherwise be even more absurd. It says, "There's expansion because there was an explosion"—the explosion of Christ bursting the bonds of death and inviting the world into his triumph. To embrace the miracle is not to embrace nonsense. In fact, it's a way to make sense of life.

Resurrection explains why the Jesus movement did not die when he did. Resurrection explains why the Jesus movement continued its unlikely growth through many deadly trials. Resurrection explains why the Victim has come to be Victor. Resurrection explains why, far from being a tragedy, the cross has represented healing and hope. Resurrection explains why the pattern of all great stories—and the pattern of the meaningful life—is triumph *through* sacrifice. Most of all, resurrection explains Jesus. It explains why the one famous for his death has been encountered by billions as the one most fully alive.

Everyone is confronted with an absurdly improbable event: Christianity rose to life to have dominion over the world. Christians say, *We have an explanation: Christianity rose to life because Christ rose to life.* And if you start leaning towards the Jesus explanation, then you can embrace the most wonderful truths:

— that the world is loved, and loved to death;

— that such love is the very essence of who God is;

— that behind the history you witness is a History Maker who can be trusted;

— that above the values you prize is a person who embodies them;

— that beneath the values you violate is the mercy to forgive you; and...

— that beyond the death you must die is the life he has pioneered: resurrection.

Unquestionably these are extraordinary ideas to embrace. But then, all ordinary ideas are off the table. We live in an utterly extraordinary world. We are the heirs of a wholly improbable history. It's a case of "choose your miracle". And if you are at all attracted to the Jesus miracle, read on for some final words of advice. If you follow them, you may just find yourself saying, "I'm amazed at my own belief, and I don't understand it".

FINAL WORDS

In the introduction I promised to speak to three kinds of reader. As we finish, let me circle back to those three audiences. I want to address the "nones" (those with no religious affiliation), the "dones" (those who feel they have moved on from Christianity), and the "won" (those who are Christians already).

TO THE "NONES": DON'T LEAP

"Of course, you know I could never share your faith." So wrote a friend of mine in a letter. She felt it was constitutionally impossible for her to believe. Many of my friends feel the same. They think that they are not people of faith and that I am. I have somehow "taken the leap"—a leap they are too sceptical or scared to take themselves.

This idea of a leap of faith is popular. Perhaps the most famous Hollywood depiction involves Indiana Jones in *The Last Crusade*. The intrepid archaeologist must cross a deep chasm and simply trust that an invisible pathway bridges it. Though he cannot see the bridge, he nevertheless steps out onto the apparent nothingness and... thud... his foot lands on something solid. The bridge exists. The leap is rewarded. Brave old Indy!

Of course, if that's what faith is, most people conclude it's not for them. It takes a bold (or stupid!) kind of person to wager their life on an invisible saviour. Most people are not the Indiana Joneses of spirituality; and so, if that is faith, then no wonder my friends say, "It's not for me".

But this is not what faith is like. And here is a deeper problem: this is not what life is like either. The "leap of faith" view assumes that most of the time we walk around on solid ground—no faith necessary. We simply live by science and reason and what can be proved under laboratory conditions. In this view, most people live a grounded, evidence-based life while a few "religious" folk choose to believe in an unproven higher plane. That's the real problem with the "leap of faith" view. And it could not be further from the truth.

If you've been following the argument of this book, you will realise that all of us live at a dizzying height. The Christianisation of our world has been history's great "leap of faith". In terms of the values that we take for granted, we are all mid-air—six miles high! Few, if any, of us can live at ground level, simply treating ourselves and our fellow humans as mischievous little apes. Our fundamental attitudes and goals assume that we and others are profoundly significant moral beings. We treat each other (or, at least, we feel we ought to treat each other) as bearers of a dignity that cannot be proved or earned. We take it on faith.

In philosopher Larry Siedentop's phrase, Christianity has

taught us to "wager on the moral equality of humans".[161] In other words, we step out into the world on the basis of prior beliefs about ourselves and others. And it's a gamble because maybe I'll treat the other person as supremely valuable, and maybe they'll treat me like a mischievous ape in return. Nevertheless, I make the wager. I live by faith. And so do you.

If you say you have no faith, I'll say, "I don't believe you". And it's not just human rights and moral equality—it's all seven WEIRD values we have explored and so much more. We are all believers already. We do not need to take a "leap of faith". Our culture has already taken an almighty leap. What we really need is some ground beneath our feet.

How do we go about finding it? A first step would be meeting your maker. (Don't worry, it's not what you might think.) You may not believe that Jesus is your Maker-with-a-capital-M, but perhaps you've seen that, through the ebbs and flows of history, he is the maker of your moral universe. So here's my advice: meet him. Meet Jesus. Read through the Gospels slowly—the biographies of Jesus in the Bible entitled Matthew, Mark, Luke and John—and see if you don't sense in Jesus a power truer and deeper than the values you're standing on: a Compassion beneath the compassion you prize; a Love beneath the love you believe in.

As you encounter the Jesus of the Gospels, ask yourself two kinds of question, one cosmic and one personal.

---

161   Larry Siedentop, *Inventing the Individual* (Penguin, 2015), p 65.

Who is Jesus at the *cosmic* level? Is he just one more figure of history, or might he be more than that? Could he be the "Son of Man" and "Son of God"—the very essence of humanity *and* of divinity? Might Jesus be what God is like: Lord of this world?

Then ask: Who is Jesus at the *personal* level? Is he trustworthy? Could you trust Jesus more than you trust yourself? Might you even consider such trust to be a glad surrender? A joyful adventure? A coming home? That is to know him as "Lord" in a personal sense.

In all this, the encouragement is not to "leap"; it's to find your feet. Jesus Christ has proved himself to be a foundation for billions. He is solid rock on which to stand.

TO THE "DONES": DON'T LEAVE

If you're a "done", you feel to some degree like you're over Christianity. You know about Christian faith. You looked into it and didn't like what you saw. Perhaps you've even been deeply involved in church in the past, but now you have moved—or you want to move—beyond it. If that's you, thank you so much for picking up this book and for getting so far. Let me assure you that I can sympathise with critiques of the institutional church. Honest Christians ought to have plenty of those, and I have an armful.

Let me list some widespread criticisms of the church, and as I do so, let me put each of them in the first person, because Christians too wrestle with these issues. Here is the point though (and you won't be surprised to hear me repeat it once again): we wrestle with them *for Christian reasons*.

If I don't like the violence of Old Testament wars, or of church history in the last 2,000 years, it's probably because I've absorbed the teachings of one who said, "Put away your sword".

If I recoil at Israel's ancient practice of slavery, it's almost certainly because I've inherited biblical notions of redemption, freedom and equality.

If I'm devastated by church abuse scandals, I'm standing *with* Christ and against the misuse of sex and power endemic to human cultures.

If I abhor instances of the church mistreating minorities, I'm assigning a sacred (and distinctly Christian) value to the weak, the poor and the oppressed.

If I consider the church to be on the wrong side of history, I'm considering history and progress in thoroughly biblical ways.

If I hate the bullish colonialism that has at times accompanied the growth of the church, I'm agreeing with profoundly Christian ideals—that rulers should serve, not dominate, and that differences should be valued, not dissolved.

I could go on.

The litany of Christian crimes is long. But notice what is happening even as I air these genuine grievances. I am holding institutional power to a higher account—an incredibly biblical impulse. What's more I'm confessing, on behalf of institutional Christianity, to some terrible behaviours. Again, such confession is deeply Christian.

And, most important of all, I'm inviting us to use standards of judgment that are particularly Christ-like. I'm holding up Jesus—"the straight line" by which we measure all that's crooked. Therefore, when the church is judged and its evils exposed, that is not an anti-Christian move. Radical reform and continual repentance is baked into Christianity—the genuine kind anyway.

John Dickson uses the analogy of a song and its singers. Jesus has given the world a beautiful song. His people have often sung it out of tune—sometimes we've been the most discordant voices of all. But the song remains good and beautiful. And if you've truly heard it, you won't be able to get it out of your head.

Lori Anne Thompson was perhaps the most prominent victim of famed Christian evangelist Ravi Zacharias. He had lived a double life such that even at his funeral in 2020, Vice President Mike Pence called him "the greatest Christian apologist of this century". In reality he had been engaged for decades in the most foul sexual, spiritual and financial abuse. Lori Anne Thompson blew the whistle on how he had abused her, but it was years before she was believed. It only came out when dogged reporting from outside the church exposed the darkness within. The betrayal Thompson felt was devastating, as she disclosed in her 2021 victim-impact statement:

> "I knew the world to be an unsafe place before I met Ravi
> Zacharias—but I yet had hope that there were some
> safe and sacred spaces. I no longer live with that hope.
> I trusted him. I trusted Christendom. That trust is

irreparably and catastrophically shattered. I yet believe Christ, even if he be not true, as he is the highest ethic I can find. They (the religious elite) stripped him, beat him mercilessly, called him all manner of names, and publicly crucified him too."[162]

Here is someone who was failed utterly by Christian leaders and institutions. But the song has held her. In a sense, the song is inescapable. If Christ can be encountered—and encountered most intensely— precisely when his so-called people disgust and dispose of you, then, as one old Scripture asks of God, "Where can I flee from your presence?" (Psalm 139:7). As Thompson has said elsewhere, "I can find no fault and no falsehood in the person of Christ ... Christendom has created refugees; whereas the Christ received them."[163]

The path forward from here looks similar to the path for the "nones": to open the Gospels and hear the song once again. At the same time it is vital to restore trust in the church, too. We can't survive with the memory of a tune. We need it sung to us. We need it embodied and lived out in front of us. But overwhelmingly the responsibility for restoring trust in the church lies with the church. Which is why I want to finish with a word to Christians.

---

162   Lori Anne Thompson victim-impact statement, 8th February 2021, https:// loriannethompson.com/2021/02/08/lori-anne-thompson-victim-impact-statement/. Accessed 14th October 2021.

163   Lori Anne Thompson, Twitter, 21st October 2020. https://twitter.com/ LoriAnneThomps2/status/1318942068979474432?s=20. Accessed 25th November 2021.

TO THE "WON": BE WEIRD

Jesus never suffered from anxiety about the size or prospects of his movement. In Matthew 5 his band of followers was small and unimpressive, and his shameful death was imminent, but his belief in global success was unshakeable. Christ's concern was not so much that his church grow (he knew it would do that); he was concerned that it be distinct.

> "You are the salt of the earth. But if the salt loses its saltiness, how can it be made salty again? It is no longer good for anything, except to be thrown out and trampled underfoot.
>
> "You are the light of the world. A town built on a hill cannot be hidden. Neither do people light a lamp and put it under a bowl. Instead they put it on its stand, and it gives light to everyone in the house. In the same way, let your light shine before others, that they may see your good deeds and glorify your Father in heaven."
> (Matthew 5:13-16)

"Salt" and "a lamp" may seem insignificant, yet, by their nature, they spread their influence far and wide. This is what the church is like. Like salt, the church will preserve—not just meat (as salt did in the ancient world), but preserve the whole earth. Like light the church will shine, illuminating the world. But salt and light are influential precisely because they are *different* from what surrounds them. Salt must be salty, and light must be bright. Salt without saltiness is worthless just as a lamp under a basket is useless. The greatest need of the church therefore is to be distinctively itself. It must not be like the meat; it must not be like the surrounding shadows.

We end on this note because the argument of this book could easily be misunderstood. After ten chapters charting the immense influence of Christianity on the world, perhaps someone will think, "The world is basically just like the church, and vice versa" (which it definitely isn't). Someone might even think, "The church should be like the world in order to have continued influence" (which it definitely shouldn't). Such conclusions completely miss how Christian influence has worked over the centuries. The church has been potent precisely when it has been peculiar. Anyone standing against the evils of their day— like gladiatorial games, or infanticide, or pederasty, or slavery—was considered crazy. And they were all the more crazy for the preaching and theology that undergirded such campaigns. Nevertheless they "let [their] light shine before others", and the peculiar proved to be potent.

This, therefore, is a call for the church to press into its distinctive strangeness. In the introduction we considered Joseph Henrich's acronym WEIRD to describe modern societies that are Western, Educated, Industrialised, Rich and Democratic. Such societies have been heavily influenced by a certain kind of Christianity. It's true that our culture is WEIRD. But as we conclude, my challenge is for the church to be *properly* weird.

A WEIRD society says it believes in equality. A properly weird church works for reconciliation and one-ness as people from *all* backgrounds come to follow Christ. A WEIRD society says it believes in compassion. A properly weird church expends itself in the cause of love. A WEIRD society says it believes in freedom. A properly weird church uses its freedoms to serve. A WEIRD society says it's committed to certain values. A properly weird church worships the Christ to whom those values belong.

In all this, great wisdom is needed to discern the Christian-*ish* values of a WEIRD culture from true Christianity. Sometimes true Christianity will sound far too "left wing", sometimes far too "right wing". Drawing on the work of historian Larry Hurtado, church leader and author Timothy Keller has pointed out that Christian communities in the 1st century were ethnically diverse and radically generous (even, at points, holding their possessions and money in a common fund).[164] This would place them very much on the left of our modern political spectrum. Equally, they passionately opposed abortion and infanticide, and kept sex firmly within male-female marriage. At this point we would dub them right-wingers.

This combination was noticed at the time. People would remark on how Christians were promiscuous with their charitable giving and stingy with their sex lives. Their money was anyone's but their bodies were not. Such views defied the classifications of their day, and they defy ours too. But they were difficult to pin down because they were not following a political program. They were not seeking to lean left or right but to follow a call from above: the call of Christ.

---

164 Timothy Keller, "Five Features That Made the Early Church Unique", The Gospel Coalition, https://www.thegospelcoalition.org/article/5-features-early-church-unique/. Accessed 14th October 2021.

And this is the call we must heed—the call we must echo in the world. The proclamation of Christ, his death and resurrection, has demonstrated its extraordinary power. The church may find itself with particular difficulties in the secularised West, but we have been here many times before. In 1925, the author G.K. Chesterton wrote of the many occasions in history when "the Church has gone to the dogs, but on each occasion, it was the dogs that died". How is this possible? "Christianity has died many times and risen again; for it had a God who knew the way out of the grave."[165]

The kingdom of Christ is unique, and not just in its unparalleled size and longevity. It's different in that while other empires rise and fall, Christ's kingdom falls and rises—repeatedly. There has always been an ebb and flow, and always in that order. Anyone concerned by the current Western ebb can look back to millennia of inspiration in back-from-the-dead revivals. But they can also look around to astonishing contemporary growth in the world today.

By 2060, Pew Research predicts that Christianity will remain the largest belief system on earth, having continued to grow as a proportion of the world's population (while atheism, agnosticism and the "nones" will shrink from 16% to 13%). Certainly the make-up of the church is shifting towards the East and the Global South, with estimates of 40% of global Christians being

---

165 G.K. Chesterton, *The Everlasting Man*, Part 2, Chapter 6. https://www. worldinvisible.com/library/chesterton/everlasting/part2c6.htm. Accessed 2nd February 2022.

African by that stage and perhaps half of China becoming Christian.[166] These developments are of immense significance (not least because of the size and importance of China), and therefore, when considering the progress of the Jesus movement, a look *around* at global Christianity is a great cause for encouragement.

But besides the look back in history and the look around at the world, we should look up to the one who knows the way out of the grave. We need not worry about the church's size or prospects. We ought not to grasp at power as though *we* are the history-makers. We should instead trust in the King of the kingdom and shine his distinctive light into the world. The future is not in our hands, nor is it in the hands of the powerful, the popular or the perverse. The government is on Christ's shoulders, and he has promised:

> *"I will build my church, and the gates of Hades will not overcome it." (Matthew 16:18)*

---

166 "The Changing Global Religious Landscape," Pew Research Center, 5th April 2017. https://www.pewforum.org/2017/04/05/the-changing-global-religious-landscape/. Accessed 2nd February 2022.

thegoodbook

COMPANY

Thanks for reading this book. We hope you enjoyed it, and found it helpful.

Most people want to find answers to the big questions of life: Who are we? Why are we here? How should we live? But for many valid reasons we are often unable to find the time or the right space to think positively and carefully about them.

Perhaps you have questions that you need an answer for. Perhaps you have met Christians who have seemed unsympathetic or incomprehensible. Or maybe you are someone who has grown up believing, but need help to make things a little clearer.

At The Good Book Company, we're passionate about producing materials that help people of all ages and stages understand the heart of the Christian message, which is found in the pages of the Bible.

Whoever you are, and wherever you are at when it comes to these big questions, we hope we can help. As a publisher we want to help you look at the good book that is the Bible because we're convinced that as we meet the person who stands at its heart—Jesus Christ—we find the clearest answers to our biggest questions.

Visit our website to discover the range of books, videos and other resources we produce, or visit our partner site www.christianityexplored.org for a clear explanation of who Jesus is and why he came.

Thanks again for reading,

Your friends at The Good Book Company

thegoodbook.com | thegoodbook.co.uk
thegoodbook.com.au | thegoodbook.co.nz | thegoodbook.co.in

WWW.CHRISTIANITYEXPLORED.ORG

Our partner site is a great place to explore the Christian faith, with powerful testimonies and answers to difficult questions.